Cambridge Elements ≡

Elements in Eighteenth-Century Connections
edited by
Eve Tavor Bannet
University of Oklahoma
Markman Ellis
Queen Mary University of London

SECRET WRITING IN THE LONG EIGHTEENTH CENTURY

Theories and Practices of Cryptology

Katherine Ellison
Illinois State University

T0364213

CAMBRIDGE
UNIVERSITY PRESS

Shaftesbury Road, Cambridge CB2 8EA, United Kingdom

One Liberty Plaza, 20th Floor, New York, NY 10006, USA

477 Williamstown Road, Port Melbourne, VIC 3207, Australia

314–321, 3rd Floor, Plot 3, Splendor Forum, Jasola District Centre,
New Delhi – 110025, India

103 Penang Road, #05–06/07, Visioncrest Commercial, Singapore 238467

Cambridge University Press is part of Cambridge University Press & Assessment,
a department of the University of Cambridge.

We share the University's mission to contribute to society through the pursuit of
education, learning and research at the highest international levels of excellence.

www.cambridge.org
Information on this title: www.cambridge.org/9781009078146

DOI: 10.1017/9781009086820

First published 2022

A catalogue record for this publication is available from the British Library.

ISBN 978-1-009-07814-6 Paperback
ISSN 2632-5578 (online)
ISSN 2632-556X (print)

Additional resources for this publication at www.cambridge.org/secretwriting

Secret Writing in the Long Eighteenth Century

Theories and Practices of Cryptology

Elements in Eighteenth-Century Connections

DOI: 10.1017/9781009086820
First published online: November 2022

Katherine Ellison
Illinois State University

Author for correspondence: Katherine Ellison, keellis@ilstu.edu

Abstract: Cryptology of the long eighteenth century became an explicit discipline of secrecy. Theorized in pedagogical texts that reached wide audiences, multimodal methods of secret writing during the period in England promoted algorithmic literacy, introducing reading practices like discernment, separation, recombination, and pattern recognition. In composition, secret writing manipulated materials and inspired new technologies in instrumentation, computation, word processing, and storage. Cryptology also revealed the visual habits of print and the observational consequences of increasing standardization in writing, challenging the relationship between print and script. Secret writing not only served military strategists and politicians; it gained popularity with everyday readers as a pleasurable cognitive activity for personal improvement and as an alternative way of thinking about secrecy and literacy.

Keywords: cryptology, secrecy, ciphers, codes, decryption

ISBNs: 9781009078146 (PB), 9781009086820 (OC)
ISSNs: 2632-5578 (online), 2632-556X (print)

Contents

1 Introduction: Cryptology before the Long Eighteenth Century and Foundational Writings

In a poem published in 1727, "The Art of Decyphering Discovered: In a Copy of Verses to a Lady, Upon Sending Her an Ænigma, Written in Cyphers," the anonymous poet documents the moment when a distinguished lady has received a love letter written in a secret, ciphered language:

> If for a while you can sit still,
> Free from your Needle and *Quadrille*,
> And spare the Time, as one may say,
> For what is neither Work nor Play;
> Of Fish and Muslin clear your Lap,
> And put on your consid'ring Cap;
> Whilst these few Figures kiss your Hand,
> And humbly beg they may be scann'd.
>
> (*ll.* 1–8)[1]

The poet here positions the decryption of this letter as an alternative to the domestic and recreational activities of needlepoint and cards. At the same time, its pursuit becomes a priority over the daily chores of cooking and mending. It is "neither Work nor Play," an employment that is unique in what it demands from its reader. It offers this recipient, this lady, an opportunity to sit and think. Further, that intellectual labor is erotic. Deciphering is pleasurable and an act of physical connection. The ciphers "kiss" her hand and call out to her to be solved. In this 1727 poem, secret writing by cipher is clearly not some cold, unemotional discipline in which only highly trained cryptanalysts, military strategists, and politicians engage. It is cerebral and sensual.

To solve the enigma, the lady must go on a hunt, which becomes a common metaphor for deciphering during the eighteenth century. "The vowels first become your prey," the poet writes (*l.* 23). John Davys notes at the beginning of *An Essay on the Art of Decyphering* (Davys, 1737) that this skill is *vaga Venatio*, an act of wandering, a hunt or chase. "We must look for the Hare, where she is not, as well as where she is," he explains (Davys, 1737, ii). While recreational metaphors appear in some cryptology instruction of the early modern period and earlier, and cryptology is at times marketed as both practical and leisurely, the eighteenth century more visibly emphasizes its association of the learning of secret writing with the welcome opportunity to do slow, concentrated mental work to sharpen one's cunning, skill, and stamina for personal improvement or self-fulfillment. The analogy of the hunt works for

---

[1] The poem has been attributed to John Davys, but this is likely because it shares a title with his 1737 *An Essay on the Art of Decyphering*.

cryptologists of the eighteenth century because it emphasizes the decryption of secret writing for survival (physical but also political), and the invention and astuteness needed to engage in it, but also introduces a new and even more compelling motivation to learn the craft: the gratification of playing a mental game for individual development. "We sometimes start the Game, where we little expected to find it," Davys notes, "but when that is once done, we are sufficiently recompenc'd by the Pleasure we take in the Pursuit" (Davys, 1737, ii). Further, that development provides connection to others.

1.1 What Is Secret Writing?

How does one distinguish secret writing from other types of writing? Is secret writing a genre, a form, or a mode, and in what material forms did secret writing manifest during the long eighteenth century? Certainly, when the techne of writing was still new, when alphabets, styles, and syntax were undergoing change, and when materialities like manuscript and print did not yet have standard formatting, the line between an intentionally secret text and one that was simply in an unfamiliar form was a fuzzy one. The literacy required by secrecy, then, is the ability to recognize when space and shape are being purposely manipulated to hide meaning. Sometimes those manipulations are obvious, such as in the case of locked letters or obvious ciphers in which letters have been replaced by symbols or numbers (see Figure 1).[2] In those cases, secret writing is certainly formal and materially experimental. More effective secret writing hides its own secrecy, pretending to be straightforward text in familiar forms and genres, such as the epistle, with recognizable, reasonable content for the rhetorical situation and genre conventions (see Figure 2). John Wilkins (1641) notes that these approaches are superior; most impressive to him, in his *Mercury; or the Secret and Swift Messenger*, are letters written in two subtly different handwriting styles, noticeable only to the practiced eye, as Francis Bacon had also described in *De dignitate and augmentis scientiarum* (1623). These intentional manipulations, which may also be multimodal (using music, gesture, visual signs, etc.) or clearly resist traditional readings of modes as well

---

[2] Jana Dambrogio, Amanda Ghassaei, Daniel Starza Smith et al., "Unlocking History through Automated Virtual Unfolding of Sealed Documents Imaged by X-ray Microtomography" *Nature Communications* 12(1184) (2021), https://doi.org/10.1038/s41467-021-21326-w. See the accompanying Letterlocking website available online at http://letterlocking.org/. Richard Fisher reported on the project in the BBC's "The Clever Folds That Kept Letters Secret" *BBC* (June 16, 2021), available online at www.bbc.com/future/article/20210616-how-the-forgotten-tricks-of-letterlocking-shaped-history. See also "Signed, Sealed, and Undelivered," a collaborative project that studies the Brienne Collection, available online at http://emlo-portal.bodleian.ox.ac.uk/collections/?catalogue=brienne-collection. Project members include Rebekah Ahrendt, Nadine Akkerman, Jana Dambrogio, Daniel Starza Smith, and David van der Linden.

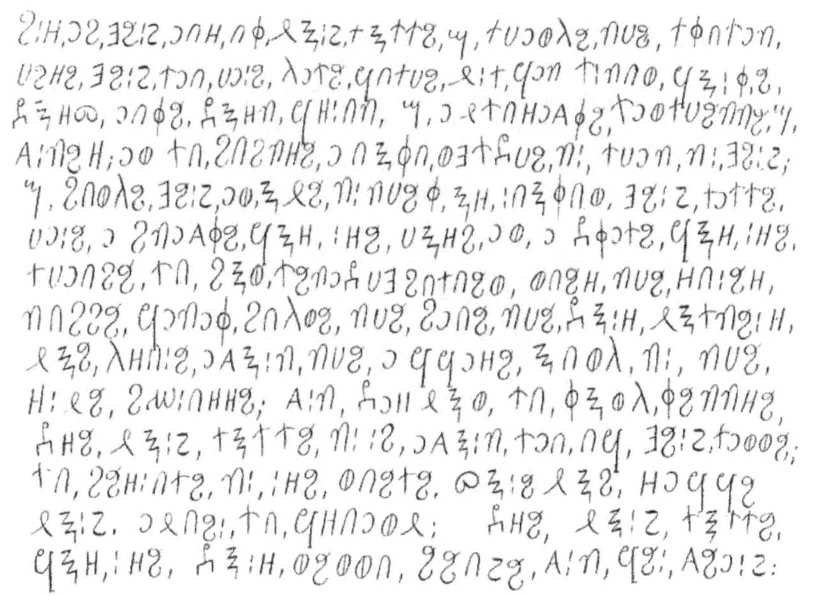

Figure 1 Obvious cipher in Gustavus Selenus's *Cryptomenytices et cryptographiae libri IX* (1624). Courtesy of the Library of Congress

as forms and genres, require a higher level of observational and situational awareness to identify even before solving. These are the subject of Section 3 of this Element. This multimodality supports Margaret Ezell's argument that late seventeenth-century English audiences demonstrated a wide range of literacies, which is also true of eighteenth-century audiences even as their alphabetic literacy expanded.[3] She looks at broadsheets to examine how audiences of varied skill levels and from a range of class and educational backgrounds were experiencing visual, oral, kinetic, and alphabetic modalities, which challenged them but also created greater accessibility to literacy. Secret writing, as a practice and also as it was taught in works like Wilkins's, "embrace[d] multiple levels of literacy" just as Ezell (2018) finds. Recent work on visual literacy is also changing scholarly appreciation of what it meant to read during the eighteenth century, with acknowledgment of the different kinds of reading required of citizens beyond the alphabetic.[4] David Cressy's 1980 benchmark,

---

[3] See early work by A. S. Collins in 1926 on how newspapers, magazines, novels, and more accessible education expanded the eighteenth-century reading public. Richard Altick challenged that evidence, arguing that a higher publication volume does not mean that the lower classes were reading. He believed that reading was still a privilege of the wealthy and academic classes. R. M. Wiles countered Altick in 1968, with an analysis of subscription lists.

[4] See Stephanie Koscak and Sandro Jung on visual literacy during the period.

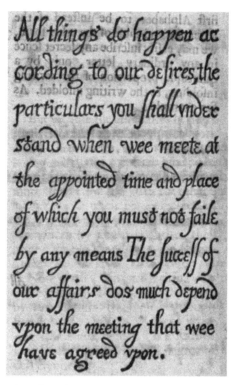

Figure 2 A cipher that disguises that it is a cipher, using a biform alphabet, in John Wilkins's *Mercury; or the Secret and Swift Messenger* (1641). This image is from the 1694 edition. Courtesy of the National Cryptologic Museum

that literacy is evidenced by whether one could sign their name, has been repeatedly challenged.

Texts that more skillfully attempted to escape suspicion are available for current analysis largely because someone, like John Wallis, identified, solved, and then shared them in diaries or collections. Often, these examples are provided in pedagogical works; for example, correspondence that Wallis collected is presented by Davys (1737) in *Art of Decyphering*. The instructional texts of the eighteenth century that focus on, or contain sections on, secret writing set out to answer these questions about intentionality while also marking the epistemological anxieties generated by not knowing whether a text is communicating a secret. Cryptography becomes an explicit *discipline* of secrecy, with genres, methods, its own history, and leading figures, to help readers determine whether or not they might in fact be encountering secret messages in their daily lives. This discipline's texts carefully outline their terms: cryptomenysis is secret information, cryptologia is secret speech, semiologia is secret visual and physical movement, like signs and gestures, and cryptography is secret writing. The term "cryptanalysis," the reading and interpretation of ciphers, did not enter the discipline's lexicon until the early twentieth century when John Matthews Manly and William F. Friedman developed an introductory handbook.[5] Cryptography is generally, but not always, obvious about the fact that it conceals a secret (see Figure 1); steganography obscures that anything is hidden, pretending honesty. Some secret writing in this Element, then, is both cryptographic and steganographic (see Figure 2).

Secret writing can take many forms, but early cryptologists agreed that secrets were most successfully communicated using codes and ciphers. Codes are, generally, straightforward equivalencies. In Daniel Defoe's code-book, discovered by Nicholas Seager, the number 92 stands for America and the number 233 refers to Queen Anne. In Defoe's use, the pairings are alphabetical as well as chronological, making it easy to figure out associations with limited knowledge. Codes are less secure than ciphers because interpretation depends upon a physically existing codebook that can be intercepted or found. King Charles I, too, typically used the same numbers for names across correspondence, so when his papers were seized at the Battle of Naseby on June 14, 1645, his letters were relatively easy for skilled decipherers to read.[6]

Ciphers, in contrast, are algorithmic and rely upon a set and sequence of instructions that may or may not be written down or recorded. Ciphers are contractual agreements between parties, as codes also are, but they require the reader or recipient to work through the message as a cognitive exercise. In other words, ciphers rely upon a relational grammar. The fourteenth-century allegorical writer Thomas Usk describes "siphers" in *The Testament of Love*, printed by William Thynne (1532) in 1532, as characters that only have power as they signify another, emphasizing the analogic, even metaphorical, nature of ciphering.[7] In this way, ciphers as ornate typographical characters, too, are clearly also related; their intricate designs obscure the plain letter and, as

---

[5] The term "cryptanalysis" was coined by John Matthews Manly, a medieval studies scholar at the University of Chicago, in consultation with William Friedman, cryptographer, in 1923. Friedman published a handbook of terms that year, "Elements of Cryptanalysis."

[6] Beáta Megyesi, Crina Tudor, Benedek Láng et al. analyze linguistic trends in cipher keys in the fifteenth through eighteenth centuries, available online, in the proceedings of HistoCrypt 2022, at https://ecp.ep.liu.se/index.php/histocrypt/index: "What Was Encoded in Historical Cipher Keys in the Early Modern Era?"

[7] Thomas Usk's *Testament of Love* was printed in William Thynne's 1532 Chaucer edition. It also appears in *Chaucerian and Other Pieces*, ed. Walter W. Skeat (Oxford: Clarendon Press, 1897), 1–145.

monograms or drop caps, only function meaningfully in relation to the text or images around them.[8] In Section 2.2, I provide several examples of how these instructions can work and the kind of thinking that they require.

William Petty's (1674) *The Discourse Made Before the Royal Society ... Concerning the Use of Duplicate Proportion* (1674) provides a helpful characterization of ciphering as the process of carving meaning from a difficult surface. To solve a cipher, then, requires not "breaking" it but manipulating its properties using a problem-solving process that recreates the situation of the message's own composition. Decipherers, who are not privy to the contractual rules, must develop methods of identifying the message's plaintext language (English, Latin, etc.), its genre, and its textual form through a trial-and-error simulation of its possible sequences. Often, decipherers use strategies like pattern and frequency analysis, which, as I explain in Section 2, will become theoretically significant as types of eighteenth-century reading practices.

1.2 Recent Explorations of Early Secret Writing

From the ancient hidden writings described by Polybius, Virgil, Cleomenes, Democritus, and Julius Africanus to cryptographic Viking, Runic, and early Irish texts and the medieval cipher systems of Isidore, the Venerable Bede, Rabanus Maurus, and Hildegard von Bingen, secret communication – or cryptomenysis – has a long, rich history that is inspiring international investigation across timelines and geographies.[9] As Elsa De Luca and John Haines (2018) note in *A Material History of Medieval and Early Modern Ciphers: Cryptography and the History of Literacy*, edited by the present author and the medievalist scholar Susan Kim, at least ninety-three medieval sources contain known cryptographic neumes. Certainly, the practice was even more widespread as well, as there is evidence of other ciphers written in material that was not sustainable over time, such as wax.

Political figures of the early modern period, too, protected their most guarded plans using cryptographic methods that scholars have only recently begun to

---

[8] The term "cipher" also refers to typographic ornamentation, including ornate monograms and large initial letters at the beginnings of paragraphs or sections, called drop caps. These often looked like puzzles, making it difficult for readers to identify the alphabetic letter. Interlocking monograms, for example, weave the letters together. They must be understood using the context of the writing in which they appear.

[9] Wilkins mentions Greek and Latin textual precedents in *Mercury* to establish the rich prehistory of secret writing, though he does not provide literature reviews of the sources. The more obscure of these, Julius Africanus, is likely Sextus Julius Africanus (ca. 180–250) who wrote encyclopedic volumes on natural history, magic, and military strategy entitled *Κεστοί* (*Charms*). He does not cite more recent medieval examples, such as Rabanus Maurus's ninth-century word images in *De laudibus sanctae crucis* (810–814), which are encrypted religious pattern poems.

examine for their cultural significance. Coded and ciphered documents authored by Queen Elizabeth, Mary, Queen of Scots, Nicholas Wotton, Sir William Pickering, Francis Walsingham, William Cecil, Nicholas Throckmorton, Sir Thomas Smith, Thomas Chaloner, John Somer, Sir Henry Cobham, Henry Norris, Thomas Randolph, John Thurloe, and Sir Edward Nicholas have all been found in the archives, revealing that the practice of secret writing was thriving before as well as during the Wars of the Three Kingdoms (1639–1651).[10] As Richard Deacon, Lois Potter, Bernard Porter, Alan Marshall, J. A. Downie, Robert Maslen, and Barbara J. Shapiro have established, espionage emerged as a government priority in England during the seventeenth century after generations of occasional but not structurally consistent systems of intelligence had been attempted. England's intelligence priorities were motivated largely by international pressures; under the Tudors, ciphered messages created a "private war" in which figures like Francis Walsingham, John Dee, and Gilbert Gifford studied past and recent cryptographic methods by Leon Battista Alberti, Gerolamo Cardano, and others to stay informed of foreign activities (Deacon, 1969, 25).

In England, local tensions then broadened conversations about secrecy, particularly during the Wars of the Three Kingdoms, the Glorious Revolution of 1688, and continued internal factions into the new century and under Georgian leadership. The seizure of Charles I's ciphered correspondence when he fled the scene at the Battle of Naseby in 1645, published as *The Kings Cabinet Opened* that same year, confirmed for the public that secret writing played an important role in the management of their nation and was also commercially successful when disclosed in print.[11] Davys references Charles I's ciphered correspondence in his first paragraph and cites other collections of ciphered messages that have yet to be examined, like Sir William Cecil's letters to Sir Henry Norris (Davys, 1737, 41). Davys notes that these letters are published in *Cabala, sive scrinia sacra*.[12] The union with Scotland, too, required espionage and, consequently, secret writing, as Defoe's correspondence shows. Defoe, who helped facilitate the union as a spy, would draft a "Scheme of General Intelligence" in a letter to Robert Harley in July or August 1704, encouraging Harley to expand his intelligence network and center

---

[10] See, for example, Edward Nicholas, *The Nicholas Papers: Correspondence of Sir Edward Nicholas, Secretary of State*, ed. George F. Warner, vol. IV, 1657–1660 (London: Office of the Society, 1920).

[11] See Charles I, *The Kings Cabinet Opened: Or, Certain Packets of Secret Letters and Papers, Written with the Kings Own Hand, and Taken in His Cabinet at Nasby-Field, June 14, 1645* (London: Printed for Robert Bostock, 1645).

[12] There are several editions of this text, but the earliest appeared during the Wars of the Three Kingdoms in 1654 and 1661. Davys might refer to a 1691 printing.

counterinsurgency espionage as a state priority.[13] And, in the early sciences, too, cryptography was useful in protecting discoveries and raising the public's curiosity. Galileo Galilei used cryptic anagrams in a message about his discovery of Saturn's moons, Tycho Brahe protected his calculation of exact longitude so complexly that it has never been solved, and Robert Boyle famously hid his research findings from his own assistants by ciphering them (Láng, 2018, 161).

Historical coverage of cryptology in the decades between Defoe and the American and French revolutions is sparse. Certainly, those revolutions ushered in yet another era of secret writing. Analysis of methods used during the American Revolutionary War is not the subject of this Element, but the University of Michigan Clements Library features a collection of twelve letters in *Spy Letters of the American Revolution* that provides a sense of wartime practices.[14] Adrienne Wilmoth Lerner, David Robarge, Russ Castronovo, Sharon Hrycewicz, Jodie Gilmore, Arnav Sharma, David Benjamin Richie, and others have provided overviews and discussion of secret writing during the revolutions. Much work, in particular, has been devoted to George Washington's interests in cryptography.

Cryptography and intelligence historians, like Deacon and David Kahn, have focused on the relative lack of "sophistication" of secret writing methods during these periods, with general dismissal of the seventeenth and eighteenth centuries as disorganized, unfocused, and uninventive. Deacon concludes that "the history of English ciphering has been characterised by its oddities and eccentricities more than any logical development of the art," and Kahn concludes that, with the exception of John Falconer's *Cryptomenysis Patefacta: Or the Art of Secret Information Disclosed without a Key* (1685), the pedagogical texts on cryptography that are the focus of this Element "shed no new light on polyalphabetics and none on the political cryptography of their day. They are divorced from the realities, and generally content themselves with commentaries on earlier works" (Deacon, 1969, 27; Kahn, 1996, 92). Further, they are the reason "people still think cryptanalysis mysterious" and "stained cryptology so deeply with the dark hues of esoterism that some of them still persist, noticeably coloring the public image of cryptology" (Kahn, 1996, 92).

It is certainly true that some experiments with cryptography by amateur secret writers lacked complexity. Defoe's use of code was rather elementary

---

[13] Robert Harley was the British Secretary of State during the reign of Queen Anne. He employed Defoe and others as spies and intelligence agents not only to gather information but also to sway public opinion.

[14] See Kate Foster, Cynthia Ghering, Michelle Light, and Melissa McCallum, "Spy Letters of the American Revolution (1763–1783)" Clements Library, University of Michigan online exhibit, available online at https://clements.umich.edu/exhibit/spy-letters-of-the-american-revolution/.

compared to the methods of secret writing taught in the texts of this Element, but he was writing quickly, without training, and he was also more successful with other forms of secret communication. For example, Defoe engaged in what he called "Publick Intelligence," which is the use of newspapers and reviews to spin information and persuade audiences (Defoe, 1704, i, 52). He would actually publish the secrets he had just obtained as a spy at the same time that he delivered ciphered messages about them to inform Harley, demonstrating how eighteenth-century writers recognized the fluidity of secrecy and publicity. Defoe's goals were certainly in line with the vision of both public and personal improvement that more trained cryptographers proposed. Across the writings of the later seventeenth century and through the eighteenth century, secrecy in communication was also linked to personal, spiritual growth. For Defoe, the circulation of secret information in the state paralleled his theological vision of how information circulates from God and an "angelic ministry" through communities and to the individual (Defoe, 1720, 225). So, while political necessity helped motivate the demand for secret writing instruction, thinkers like Defoe were also inspired by a vision of universal connectivity. Sarah Myers West calls this the "cryptographic imaginary" or the "networked public," but I would go further to emphasize the human connection that is central to secret writing as a mode of communication at this time.[15]

News reports of discovered secret writings still intrigue readers today. In August 2021, staff at the Bodleian Library shared online a 1746 ciphered letter to Thomas Villiers, later 1st Earl of Clarendon; more frequently, libraries are publicly announcing when they find ciphers, keys, or documents in need of decryption.[16] In October 2020, Dominic Winter Auctioneers sold fifty-three letters from a 1653 volume, deciphered by John Wallis, for $37,000 (Taub, 2020). Karen Britland, Sarah Poynting, Nadine Akkerman, Benedek Láng, Philip Beeley, Christoph Scriba, Karl de Leeuw, Jan Bergstra, and others have contributed significant perspectives on these ciphered correspondences. Emerging scholars are also interested in ciphering, such as V. M. Braganza, who identified a coded monogram on a seventeenth-century binding as belonging to Lady Mary Wroth.[17] The discovery was excitedly reported in *Fine*

---

[15] Sarah Myers West (2018), Cryptographic Imaginaries and the Networked Public, *Internet Policy Review*, 7(2), available online at https://policyreview.info/articles/analysis/cryptographic-imaginaries-and-networked-public.

[16] See "Secret Ciphers," Bodleian Archives and Manuscripts blog, August 8, 2021, available online at https://blogs.bodleian.ox.ac.uk/archivesandmanuscripts/2021/08/02/secret-ciphers/.

[17] Proving the continued public interest in ciphering, Braganza's *English Literary Renaissance* article was immediately reported on by the magazine writer Rebecca Rego Barry, "A 17th-Century Monogrammed Binding Reveals Its Secrets" *Fine Books & Collections*, January 2022, available online at www.finebooksmagazine.com/blog/17th-century-monogrammed-binding-reveals-its-secrets.

Books & Collections magazine and circulated on social media in January 2022. Currently, a team including Láng and Beáta Megyesi is developing a historical cipher database, DECODE, as well as a repertoire of tools, DECRYPT, so that scholars can upload, share, and decipher documents they find.[18] An international organization, HistoCrypt, has gathered annually since 2016 to bring together historians, computer scientists, and mathematicians to share new knowledge on coded and ciphered writings from the past.[19]

This Element focuses on cryptography of the long eighteenth century, which, with the exception of the American Revolutionary War, has received less attention than the medieval and early modern periods, and on the English tradition of *teaching* secret writing in the period after central Europe's Thirty Years' War of 1618–1648 and the Wars of the Three Kingdoms. It also provides an emphasis on teaching to signal a shift in the motivation for secret writing away from only protecting one's situation, politics, or craft and toward doing so as a process of personal growth and self-education. In a sense, this is when cryptology, as the study of secret communication, began as a discipline. This was a period when hiding one's written thoughts remained a practical method of personal and national security but also began to be historicized, analyzed, and then theorized in print publication as a new framework for modern, multimodal, multilinguistic literacy to better oneself. In short, cryptographers became reflectively aware of secret writing as *having* a history and of secrecy as a significant and productive framework in human communication, literacy, and identity.

1.3 Secret Writing Instruction during the Long Eighteenth Century

Important in this transition was the disengagement of cryptography from the occult and recognition of it as a discipline in its own right, with a history, methods, serious practitioners, and public and private utility. This entailed gathering together and summarizing ancient and recent accounts of and references to secret writing. Wilkins's (1641) *Mercury; or the Secret and Swift Messenger*, the first full manual written in English, is one of the early comprehensive attempts (Figure 3). It surveys Greek, Roman, biblical, and more recent examples, though with obvious historical gaps. It includes (brief) references to

---

[18] DECRYPT provides tools for collecting and solving historical ciphers by using AI, and the DECODE database (available online at https://doi.org/10.1080/01611194.2020.1716410) provides a way of collectively sharing documents as scholars find them. Teams from several European universities and organizations are currently developing the CrypTool Portal, which will provide tools for semi-automatic transcription and decryption of early modern and modern ciphers. See Beáta Megyesi, Bernhard Esslinger, Alicia Fornés et al., "Decryption of Historical Manuscripts: The DECRYPT project" *Cryptologia* 44(6) (2020).

[19] Information about HistoCrypt is available online at https://histocrypt.org.

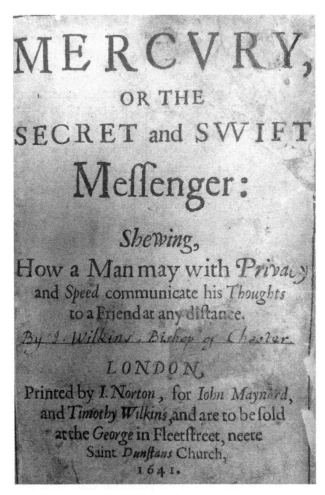

Figure 3 Title page of John Wilkins's *Mercury; or the Secret and Swift Messenger* (1641). Courtesy of the National Cryptologic Museum

Jewish, Egyptian, Middle Eastern, and other European practices and connects the history of secret communication to the history of writing itself, emphasizing that writing is mysterious, even seemingly like magic, when one does not know how it works. Rhetorically strategic, Wilkins cites many classical examples to prove that secret communication had changed history, linking that type of literacy to a legitimate, practical cultural purpose. He is knowledgeable of important sixteenth-century instruction, too, from Girolamo Cardano's (Jérôme Cardan) *De subtilitate rerum* (1550) to Giambattista della Porta's (Giovanni Battista Della Porta) *De furtivis literarum notis* (1563), though he does not indicate whether he had read them closely. With nods toward his own generation's contributions, like Francis Bacon's arguments for protected know-ledge in *De dignitate and augmentis scientiarum* (1623) and description of the biliteral cipher, Francis Godwin's *Nuncius inanimatus* (1629), which inspired Wilkins's interest in musical ciphers, and Gustavus Selenus's (1624) *Cryptomenytices et cryptographiae libri IX*, which helped dismantle the allegedly occult influences of Johannes Trithemius's sixteenth-century work, Wilkins establishes a corpus for the serious discussion of secret writing.[20] He mentions, too, Trithemius's *Polygraphiae libri sex* (1518) and *Steganographia* (circulated in 1499), which had seen renewed interest since the republication of several sixteenth-century works on cryptography and after Selenus simplified the solutions to ciphers in *Steganographia*'s Books I and II, proving that they were indeed functional. With this foundational work established, Wilkins then steps through a range of instructional examples, from simple to more complex, with emphasis on the superior security of multimodal methods, like the biform alphabet (using two different handwriting styles or scripts, such as italic and nonitalic, in which one is a decoy), ciphering using images, and ciphering using sound and music. *Mercury* lays the groundwork for all later English instruction in secret writing. It appeared in three editions, and most secret writing texts reference it or copy full sections.

In the 1650s and 1660s, notable secret writing instruction was provided by several texts: a preface written by John Wallis in 1659 (but not published until 1737), Noah Bridges's (1659) *Stenographie and Cryptographie*, an anonym-ously published response to Bridges's (1665) work entitled *Rarities: Or the Incomparable Curiosities in Secret Writing* (previously thought to have been authored by Bridges), and Samuel Morland's (1666) *A New Method of Cryptography*. Wallis's preface was not published until 1737, so it will be examined in this Element when I discuss John Davys's inclusion of it in *An Essay on the Art of Decyphering*. Bridges's work is unique in its attention to transmutation, which is the use of a symbolic system to express magnitude; cryptography becomes a linguistically as well as numerically experimental way to express experience as it occurs on a massive scale. Scientifically, and theologically, this is tied to deliberations about the relation between bodies in the universe and the ability of human language to communicate that immensity. Codes, ciphers, and even shorthand provide a kind of relief for the

---

[20] Gustavus Selenus was a pseudonym for Augustus of Brunswick-Lüneburg (or, August, Duke of Braunschweig-Lüneburg). Johannes Trithemius was a pseudonym for Johann Heidenberg. Like Trithemius's *Polygraphiae libri sex* (1518), John Dee's work in cryptography was also accused of occultism. Dee's earlier ciphers, in diaries, letters, and *The Monad, Hieroglyphically, Mathematically, Magically, Cabbalistically, and Analogically Explained* (1564), communicated information through chemical symbols, aligning cryptography with alchemy and inviting readers to reject his methods as "mumbo-jumbo" (Deacon, 1969, 29).

overwhelming, often traumatic, excesses of early modern culture – civil wars, political division, natural disasters, scientific discoveries that challenge religious belief, and more. Bound with *Stenographie* in one copy in the Bodleian Library, hence the assumption of its serial nature and authorship, the anonymous *Rarities* appears to be, at least in part, a critique of *Stenographie*. It emphasizes the accessibility of cryptography to novices, stressing that more than mathematical education or the ability to memorize complex instructions, secret writing demands the creativity of a mind that can be nimble and spontaneous. Even its title, which markets secret writing as a rarity and a curiosity, contrasts with Bridges's more technical title.

Morland's *New Method* is a kind of anomaly in the publication history of secret writing. Unlike the others of that generation, it was not published for the general public but for the court of Charles II. Only a few copies appear to exist or survive, and it is not mentioned in any later historical overviews. Yet, it is arguably the most technically important pamphlet, printed in color and with original approaches to secret writing using highly mathematical and geometric methods. It also recommends technological assistance and the development of a repertoire of instruments to make both ciphering and deciphering faster and more accurate.

From the 1680s through the eighteenth century, publications explicitly about secret writing were highly intertextual, referencing past publications and adding some new methods to intrigue readers. Instructional manuals of the later seventeenth century, in particular, present a kind of practical counterpart to the secret histories that were popular at the time, such as the translation of Procopius's *Anekdota* (ca. 550), published in English as *Secret History of the Court of the Emperor Justinian* (1674).[21] More than 400 works during the seventeenth and eighteenth centuries include "secret history" in their titles in the English Short Title Catalogue alone, and scholarship in the past twenty years has provided rich commentary on the complexities of these publications and of the connected genres of books of secrets. Allison Kavey's (2007) *Books of Secrets: Natural Philosophy in England, 1500–1600* updates the foundational work of William Eamon, who in 1994 published *Science and the Secrets of Nature: Books of Secrets in Medieval and Early Modern Culture*. Eamon is most interested in how medieval "how to" books of the occult founded modern science. Kavey revises Eamon's research and focuses on the popular audience as target readership for early modern books of secrets, arguing that "these books presented readers with models of the natural world that were susceptible to

---

[21] See Peter Burke, "Publicizing the Private: The Rise of 'Secret History,'" in *Changing Perceptions of the Public Sphere*, ed. Christian J. Emden and David Midgley (New York, NY, 2012), 67–69.

human manipulation, pointed to the agents of natural change that were vulnerable to such efforts, and issued instructions for producing particular change that would suit or satisfy human desires" (Kavey 2007, 3). Rebecca Bullard and Rachel Carnell's (2017) *The Secret History in Literature, 1660–1820* and Peter Burke's (2016) *Secret History and Historical Consciousness: From Renaissance to Romanticism* explain the literary, historical, and political significance of the secret history as a genre during the eighteenth century. Bullard and Carnell approach secret histories from a literary studies point of view with focus on genre, authorship, and storytelling, while Hofstadter and Burke look to secret histories as they signal a new kind of political thought characterized by paranoia, suspicion, and distrust. Nonfiction publications on cryptography are not secret histories, but they do share their appeal to reader excitement and curiosity, the promise to reveal secrets, and capitalization upon a paranoid reading culture. At times, instructional cryptography texts even structurally follow some of the conventions of fictional plots that hinge on secrets hidden and discovered. Brian Cowan notes that early modern books of secrets are interesting, in part, because like novels, they engage with contemporary anxieties about fact and fiction. Together, secret histories and secret writing pedagogy flourished as what Bullard describes as "polemical forms of historiography" (Cowan, 2016, 137).

The polemical nature of cryptography instruction, and its self-reflective understanding of changing literacies in the more global economies and increasingly polarized politics of the approaching eighteenth century, are precisely what cryptography historians have missed in their surveys of the period. Kahn dismisses most later seventeenth- and eighteenth-century cryptography texts as esoteric and practically useless, excepting only Falconer's *Cryptomenysis* because it mentions columnar transposition. Kahn notes that, overall, the publications are "all theory and no practice" (Falconer, 1996, 92). But that theory is significant. Several of Falconer's methods will be discussed in the next sections, particularly those that involve the material handling of texts and manipulation of their surfaces and structures. Like Falconer's *Cryptomenysis*, Charles La Fin's (1692) *Sermo Mirabilis: Or the Silent Language* also seeks alternatives to alphabetic writing to communicate in secret. La Fin will contribute to contemporary scholarship in literacies for the physically disabled.

While the volume of publications about secret writing after the turn of the eighteenth century does not exceed the previous century, the nature and focus of the publications do change after Falconer and La Fin. There are some manuals that try to be similar to the early modern predecessors, like James Swaine and Joseph Simms's (1761) *Cryptography: Or a New, Easy, and Compendious System of Short-Hand, Adapted to All the Various Arts, Sciences, and Professions.*

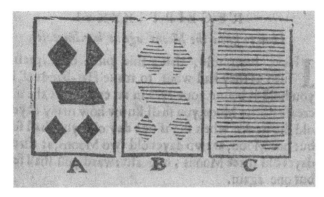

Figure 4 Example secret writing method in John White's (1704) *A Rich Cabinet of Modern Curiosities*. Courtesy of the Library of Congress. Digital image: https://hdl.loc.gov/loc.rbc/Rosenwald.1527

This text, though, misuses the term "cryptography" and is essentially a grammar textbook entirely on shorthand. More common were publications on other subjects that included sections on secret writing. Richard Neve cites both Wilkins's *Mercury* and Falconer's (1702) *Cryptomenysis* in *Apopiroscopy: Or, a Compleat and Faithful History of Experiments and Observations* in a lengthy section on secret writing using invisible, disappearing, and glowing inks. John White's (1704) *A Rich Cabinet of Modern Curiosities* includes advice on writing secret letters to best friends and lovers (Figure 4). Andrew Dunton's (1705) *Dunton's Wit's Exercise*, a fashionable compendium of novel curiosities, allegories, riddles, and secrets, has two very short sections on ciphering, with examples but no clear explanations. These kinds of inclusions are clearly presented for superficial entertainment only, staged as brainteasers to improve the reader's "wit," but I see that focus as indicative of the pervasive eighteenth-century rhetorical positioning of cryptography as measure of – and self-directed bolster of – intelligence. John Wilkes's (1799?) *The Art of Making Pens Scientifically*, which notes in its subtitle that it contains *Also, Directions for Secret Writing*, is likewise for readers who fashion themselves as developing intellectuals. Yet, it is also interested in secret writing for another purpose. As I explain in more detail in Section 2 on cipher devices, Wilkes aligns ciphering with a local, nonindustrial and preprint past of handcrafted instruments. Overall, though, these publications demonstrate how popular, and personally useful, secret writing had come to be during the eighteenth century. Nonprofessional cryptographers favored easy yet effective, do-it-yourself material means of circulating secrets over complex ciphers, such as mixing invisible inks and cutting holes in paper (see Figure 4).

In this method, the sender and receiver share identical papers with holes cut into them, layered over a full sheet below. The secret message is written in the spaces of the holes. Then, the top "key" paper is removed, and the writer fills in the rest of the page with either nonsense words or words that appear to create a separate, decoy message. The recipient lays their identical key paper on top to reveal the plaintext.

Robert More's (1716) *Of the First Invention of Writing* references Bacon and Falconer and copies sections from Wilkins's *Mercury*, but despite Wilkins's work to disassociate cryptography from the occult, More explicitly defines cryptography *as* "Occult Writing" and refers to secret writing, throughout his text, as an occult practice (More 1716, 5). More's subject is the history and practice of writing, more generally, so secret writing is a short section. He summarizes publications on the practice of writing studies as a discipline, and on composition and handwriting instruction, showcasing the burgeoning of the field since the 1590s and with a shifting focus toward the thought processes that writing entails. More's text marks a transitional moment in the teaching of writing: it explicitly frames writing as the visual manifestation of cognition – and of the imagination – as channeled through the physical, material movement of the body. I go into more detail about More's demonstrations of this movement in Section 4 on cryptotypographies.

Most significant from the period are two longer publications dedicated entirely to secret writing: *An Essay on the Art of Decyphering* (Davys, 1737), framed and edited by John Davys, and Philip Thicknesse's (1772) *A Treatise on the Art of Decyphering and of Writing in Cypher*. Davys's *Art of Decyphering* creates a kind of celebrity portrait of the seventeenth-century cryptographer John Wallis, who had died in 1703. Wallis was employed as a decipherer first by Cromwell, then by Charles II, and finally by William and Mary. Davys's dense exposition centers Wallis in a network and legacy of deciphering, articulating the historical and cultural significance of the interpretative processes of solving ciphers. It is not explicitly about secret writing, though understanding methods of writing is necessary to delve more deeply into the ways in which ciphering has changed reading. By the publication of *Art of Decyphering*, ciphers were not only circulating in published collections of correspondence, such as the 1742 publication of *A Collection of the State Papers of John Thurloe*, and playing a significant role in Georgian politics, but they were also on public trial in famous court cases. Secret messages were presented as evidence, and verdicts of guilt or innocence came down to how the messages were deciphered and by whom.[22] There is indication in Davys's rhetoric that the power and authority of

---

[22] See Thomas Birch, *A Collection of the State Papers of John Thurloe, Esq; Secretary, First, to the Council of State, and Afterwards to the Two Protectors, Oliver and Richard Cromwell. In Seven Volumes* (London, 1742).

secret writing was being challenged; cryptography was losing its reputation as a credible technical discipline under intense political and legal scrutiny. The contemporary texts just mentioned, with sections on secret writing alongside other curiosities and entertainments, were perhaps eroding its seriousness as a craft with logical, verifiable technical methods. There were even revived accusations of occult influences. Davys's inclusion of a preface Wallis had written for his own collection of letters, which Wallis did not go on to publish, bookended by Davys's explanations and analysis, helps him to at once remind the public of the intellectual rigor necessary to *do* cryptanalysis yet still include the novice reader as a student with potential. Learning decryption, with Wallis as inspiration, is a way of gaining self-discipline, patience, stamina, creativity, and wit under pressure.

Thicknesse's *Treatise* is also concerned about the sinking reputation of ciphering and deciphering. He notes that even in the late eighteenth century, there are educated and intelligent persons who do not believe that deciphering is a true craft and that it is possible to read ciphered messages. They assume that deciphering is only approximation or guessing and that decipherers "pass themselves off as Men who possess an Art, not to be acquired" (Thicknesse, 1772, viii). The sense that cryptology was an occult practice must have endured throughout the eighteenth century and with some renewed fashion in the 1770s when Thicknesse was writing, because he pauses to exclaim at the ridiculousness of the reality that so many educated persons of government and law continue to discredit cryptography and cryptanalysis as black magic. Insulting the Scots, the Welsh, and the poor, Thicknesse muses that while he can understand why the uneducated and the impoverished cling to superstitions and belief in the occult and are easily manipulated by claims of magic, there is no excuse for magistrates and men of rank (Thicknesse, 1772, 15–16). Thicknesse stresses that he is neither expert nor innovator but capable of "leading those who doubt it"; importantly, he argues that deciphering is a "rational Exercise for the mind" – it is a habit of thinking that is beneficial to all readers (and especially young people, he notes), even if they do not have any real purpose for deciphering in their daily lives. The appeal of deciphering by the late eighteenth century is that it provides a "methodical Way of thinking, on any one Subject" (Thicknesse, 1772, ix). The mind that is trained in rational, step-by-step thinking when young, he emphasizes, becomes a stronger mind when aged. It is beyond the scope of this study to summarize Thicknesse's politics, but his views and methods were certainly challenged. In one caricature printed in 1790, Thicknesse's nude body is shown in dissection, its parts labeled with words like "extortion," "deceit," "inquisition," and "libel" (see Figure 5). "Genius" is written across his groin.

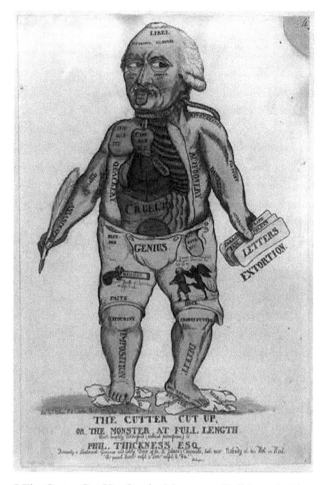

Figure 5 The Cutter Cut Up, Or, the Monster at Full Length. Photograph. Courtesy of the Library of Congress, www.loc.gov/item/2002714821/

False binaries of thinking about secrecy, and assumptions that secrecy is the opposite of transparency, openness, or even truth, as well as the association of secrecy with subversion, betrayal, and lies, began to be publicly debated and resituated, rhetorically. Cryptographers of this period posit secret writing as more truthful, more authentic (but not fully truthful or authentic) than messages that pretend transparency. Clearly, as the cartoon of Thicknesse reveals, not everyone was in agreement. By the eighteenth century, in England, however, secrecy was seen as necessary for a successful state *and* a highly functioning individual. Pedagogues of cryptography focused on *how* to behave in this inevitable culture of secrecy, with particular attention to how to write and read those secrets.

2 Ciphering and Deciphering As Writing and Reading Processes

English cryptologists had already articulated their roots in Greek and Roman cryptography and established their craft as a legitimate technical discipline by the late seventeenth century. More significantly, the instructional texts of Wilkins and the generation after him, similar to but also distinctly different from other publications that boasted access to secrets, changed how writers with secrets thought about their compositions. Though they were similar in structure to writing and penmanship manuals that had been popular since the sixteenth century, and then would influence writing instruction of the eighteenth century, cryptography instruction was concerned less with refinement and perfection of conventionalized gestures and more with recognizing the creative, spontaneous decision-making necessary to understand secrets in (often, but not always) urgent situations. Lois Potter argues in the foundational *Secret Rites and Secret Writing: Royalist Literature 1641–1660* that ciphering was culturally significant enough by the later seventeenth century that it even changed "part of the consciousness of the period" and "had more than a metaphorical meaning" (Potter, 1989, 38–39). Mary Baine Campbell identifies this same generation as a culture of "paranoid reading" (Campbell, 1999, 3). This section explores the specific ways in which cryptography changed that consciousness and addressed that paranoia over the next decades, with attention to encryption, as a method of writing, which promoted discernment through categorization and deconstructive grammar, and decryption, as a method of reading, which relied upon pattern recognition and heightened awareness of global languages. Together, secret writing instruction publications of the long eighteenth century cultivated *algorithmic literacy*.

2.1 Cryptology As Algorithmic Thinking

An algorithm is a process or set of rules by which one engages in solving a problem. In current computing contexts, the instructions are typically finite and lead to a limited number of states that produce a single outcome. These are programmed into devices so that they become responsive and automatic. Used in mathematics since Greek work on prime numbers and the thirteen books of Euclid's *Elements* (ca. 300 BC), in which he provided instructions for reducing fractions to their simplest forms, algorithms were adapted in cryptography at least as early as al-Kindi's thirteenth-century experiments in pattern analysis to break codes. The philosophical motivation for algorithmic problem solving was awareness that the physical human body and mind cannot manage the volume of information in the universe, which thinkers were facing as they pondered the scale of space or the infinitesimal smallness of atoms and molecules. Clearly, the scientific method, with its steps and rules for inquiry, is a related approach. To manage problems with seemingly limitless possibilities, thinking itself needed to be conceived of as representable in material terms, as something that can be divided into steps, externalized, witnessed, adapted, and repeated.

Secret writing manuals externalize the writing and reading processes, making materially visible, as a series of moves, the thinking necessary to hide and to disclose secrets. This is not unique to this genre, of course. Writing instruction manuals, more broadly, were also reframing the teaching of composition as algorithmic and emphasizing that by breaking such a complex skill into steps, it could make visible the thinking process and improve communication. This is rhetorically situated as a natural consequence of the materiality and visibility of writing itself, of writing as externalized thinking. Robert More, in *Of the First Invention of Writing: An Essay*, explains that writing makes thoughts visible, and these thoughts are communicated in writing through a "Connexion of Audible Signs" (More, 1716, 1). As Christopher Goodey finds is true of other writings during the eighteenth century, this instruction marks a significant shift in the consciousness of thinking as an act that can be represented and plotted through time; as a consequence, it reveals that intellectual ability can *change* with intention, practice, and access to education and resources.

In More's *First Invention*, writing is inherently algorithmic: it is endlessly adaptable through combination, variation, multiplication, and transposition, and one cannot understand a text's meaning unless they are privy to the rules of that particular assemblage. As evidence, he copies an example from Wilkins's *Mercury; or The Secret and Swift Messenger*. In this moment in *Mercury*, Wilkins is discussing how writing itself appears to be secret, and mysterious, to cultures like the "late discovered *Americans*," who do not practice it or to anyone to whom writing is a new experience. In his anecdote, a slave is asked to deliver figs to a buyer and carries a receipt for the purchase (Wilkins, 1641, 5).[23] On the first delivery, he eats some figs and is then punished when the buyer looks at the receipt and compares it against the number of figs in the basket. On the second delivery, the slave hides the receipt beneath a rock so it cannot witness his theft. But again, he is

---

[23] Anecdotes play an interesting role in secrecy during the period. An "anecdote" was a secret occurrence or circumstance of history that had been omitted or suppressed by earlier historians. See April London, "Secret History and Anecdote," in *The Secret History in Literature, 1660–1820*, eds. Rebecca Bullard and Rachel Carnell (Cambridge: Cambridge University Press, 2017), 174–187, 176.

punished. For Wilkins, this expresses the wonder of writing when it is unfamiliar; all writing is, at some point, secret writing. More references the anecdote to reveal how a reader must know the *rules* and *steps* required to decipher that writing. Even if this messenger knew the alphabet, he must also have known how it is here assembled, how the genre of the invoice works, what the numbers refer to, and how they compute. So, for More, the difference is not that writing has *become* algorithmic but that he and his contemporaries are now conscious of it. This anecdote also suggests that the messenger *can* learn the language if he learns the rules.[24]

Interestingly, Philip Thicknesse references this same anecdote in the later *A Treatise on the Art of Decyphering and of Writing in Cypher* (Thicknesse, 1772). Thicknesse changes the main character from a Native American slave to a "negro" and modifies the story. In his version, a young African slave notices that he is always punished when he carries a paper to his master. He asks the master why he is punished, and the master says that the paper talks to him and tells him the boy has been lazy. The boy then challenges him, noting that he never sees the master doing any labor, and the master explains that he works with his mind, not his body. The next time the boy is to deliver a paper ordering his punishment, he discards it. He explains that he, too, used his mind for labor (Thicknesse, 1772, 55). Though the telling is notably different, reflecting the different economic and political colonial culture of 1772 in contrast to Wilkins's 1641 and More's 1716 contexts, it still frames writing as the materialization of intelligence and emphasizes the way in which access to the rules of writing – how it works, what it means, and so forth – is tied to power. Secrecy is power, and so too is the ability to uncover and then exploit that secret.

Arguably, these algorithmic conventions are evident in – and perhaps significantly influenced by – earlier writing instruction texts, such as publications for secretaries that began appearing during the sixteenth century. In

---

[24] In *A Cultural History of Early Modern English Cryptography Manuals*, I analyze this anecdote more fully, with attention to Wilkins's economic and global trade ambitions. Certainly, Wilkins's account of the story emphasizes that writing is inevitably, and even originally, an act of imperial control, as Jonathan Goldberg notes is common in early modern writing manuals; it is the trader's means of asserting and maintaining power over Indigenous resources which he does not have a right to claim, and the messenger recognizes in writing that oppressive authority and attempts to fight against the imperial system by learning about it. Here, it is noteworthy that this anecdote, which appears across a number of writing manuals like More's, links colonial enslavement and exploitation to the cognitive processes that writing reveals. Goldberg examines Richard Mulcaster's *The First Part of the Elementarie* (1582), which depicts writing as "an imperializing gesture." Jonathan Goldberg, *Writing Matter: From the Hands of the English Renaissance* (Stanford, CA: Stanford University Press, 1990), 27.

England, Angel Day's foundational *The English Secretarie* (1586) was printed and in circulation. Nicholas Faunt's *Discourse Touching the Office of Principall Secretarie of Estate etc.* (1592) and Robert Beale's *Instructions for a Principall Secretarie, Observed by R. B. for Sir Edwarde Wotton* (1592) were in manuscript form with more limited audiences. John Herbert's memorandum, "Duties of a Secretary" (1600), and Robert Cecil's draft of "The State and Dignitie of a Secretarie of State" (1600, published in 1642) also categorized the duties of this political position and provided instruction. Francis Walsingham compiled his notes on secretarial organization, genres, and records as a table book that was then added to by his own secretaries after his death in 1590.[25] Handbooks that taught the management of secrets were also published during the eighteenth century and continued to teach writing and reading skills as algorithmic, like Thomas Goodman's *The Experience'd Secretary: Or, Citizen and Countryman's Companion* (1707) and *The Young Secretary's Guide: Or, a Speedy Help to Learning* (1718).

One also sees this consciousness of algorithmic thinking in texts that emphasized self-improvement, like *The Expert Orthographist* (1704), *Right Spelling Very Much Improved* (1704), and Joshua Oldfield's (1707) *An Essay Towards the Improvement of Reason: In the Pursuit of Learning, and Conduct of Life*. "Gentleman's" primers, too, contained sections on writing that provide algorithmic instructions and, through this, promise that men can improve themselves, like William Darrell's *The Gentleman Instructed, in the Conduct of a Virtuous and Happy Life* (1725) and George Fisher's *The Instructor: Or, Young Man's Best Companion. Containing Spelling, Reading, Writing, and Arithmetick, in an Easier Way Than Any Yet Published* (1737).

It is beyond the scope of this Element to look more broadly at the many textual and philosophic influences that promoted algorithmic thinking before and during the eighteenth century. Certainly, the rise of technical and scientific writing during the late seventeenth century also set the stage for the writing of thought processes as a series of steps, choices, and intentions. Examples, diagrams, and detailed comparison of methods, as John Bender and Michael Marrinan (2010) illustrate in *The Culture of Diagram*, had become a way of communicating new findings in mathematics, biology, astronomy, and chemistry as well as early linguistics. Secret writing, as a skill set, was no exception.

---

[25] See also the foundational Venetian secretary manual, Francesco Sansovino's *Il Secretario* (1564).

2.2 Ciphering and Deciphering As Word Processing

Cryptologists thought of language in the same way that astronomers thought of the universe, as a space of infinite possibility. Even further variation is introduced when working across the world's languages, ancient and modern. The vastness of this linguistic possibility is positioned against the alleged simplicity of the single-language world of Adam and Eve before the "curse" of multilingualism.[26] Frustration with this multiplicity, and with the impossibilities of interpretation, led Wilkins and others to propose universal language schemes that would reduce human communication to a formula. Universal language schemes were not successful, but cryptography, through its focus on the reorganization of writing and reading processes as a sequence of steps, had a larger impact on literacy practices and, obviously, the political and economic future of England.

Approaching written language as an expansive space of possibilities, and secret writing as itself even more capacious, Morland, Bridges, and other cryptologists emphasize the overwhelming scale of information involved in making sense of their ciphers. Morland notes that there are "millions of millions of distinct orders" in the methods he outlines, making it impossible for anyone to solve his ciphers without strict adherence to the instructions he provides (Morland, 1666, 7). To help the reader understand that the demands of interpretation for his generation now face more variations than are humanly possible to solve without the aid of algorithmic approaches, he calculates that even when a message written in the English alphabet is only eighty-one letters long, arranged neatly in nine columns and nine rows, there are 373,705,000 different possible transpositions of letters. Change the method of encryption and decryption, and that same message could have up to 10,888,869,450,418,352,160,768,000,000 possibilities.[27] John Falconer makes the same point in *Cryptomenysis*, explaining that with a twenty-four-letter alphabet, "a thousand Million of Men in as many years could not write down all those different Transpositions of the Alphabet, granting every one should compleat forty Pages a day, and every Page containing forty several Positions" (Falconer, 1685, 5). Not all of those transpositions would make grammatical sense, of course, but Morland believes that no reader, no matter how skilled, could know how to start that reading without using a sequence of steps. What they need is a word processing system.

Morland begins immediately with an instruction set to reveal his *New Method of Cryptography* (1666) (see Video 1 for a demonstration).

---

[26] Wilkins, Falconer, and others use this rhetorical contrast to lament the loss of communication that resulted from the world's multiple languages.

[27] Ibid., 4.

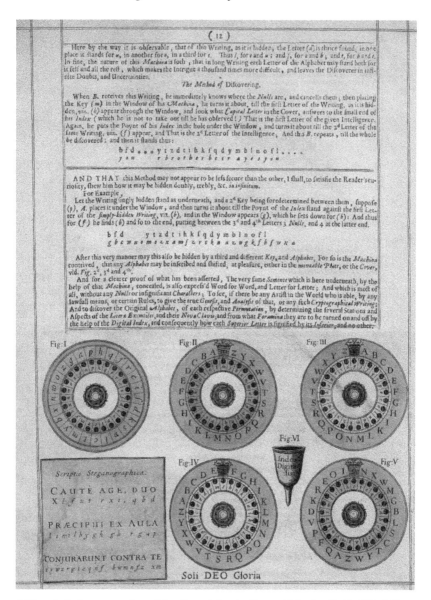

Video 1 A demonstration of the first cipher in Samuel Morland's (1666) *A New Method of Cryptography*. Images used by permission of the Folger Shakespeare Library. Video available at www.cambridge.org/secretwriting

The reader must first turn to page five (Figure 6) to find a diagram and a key (what Morland calls a Clavis Universalis and a Numeric Alphabet) which readers can, when they are ready to decipher on their own, use as templates.

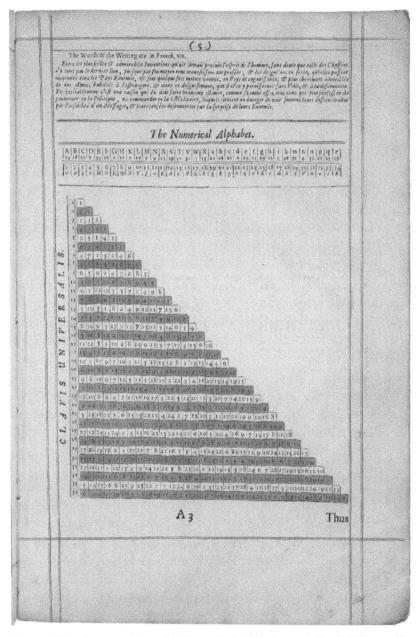

Figure 6 Starting template, with Numerical Alphabet and Clavis Universalis, for solution to cipher method in Samuel Morland's (1666) *A New Method of Cryptography*. STC M2781A, page 5, digital image 60227, used by permission of the Folger Shakespeare Library

Table 1 First key for Samuel Morland (1666) cipher in
A New Method of Cryptography

A	B	C	D	E	F	G	H	K	L	M	N	R	S	T	V	W	X
14	28	15	8	34	16	6	27	7	17	5	9	13	29	10	30	1	25
a	b	c	d	e	f	g	h	i	k	m	n	o	p	q	r		
12	18	26	2	24	11	19	22	3	20	31	4	32	21	23	33		

This template has thirty-four rows that increase columns by one. It also has a key of thirty-four capital and lower-case alphabetic letters, each paired with a number in Table 1.

In a much simpler cipher, this Numeric Alphabet alone would be all one uses. But Morland's goal here is heightened security. This key is only one step in the algorithm. The writer must work alongside their future correspondent to decide upon the arrangement of their letters and numbers in that template. Their next decisions are the length by which they will divide their message, the number of nulls they will include at the beginning and end of the message, and the direction in which the recipient must read – ascending horizontally, descending vertically, ascending diagonally, and so forth.

Some of these decisions may be made ahead of time, especially the direction in which to read, but once the intended reader understands the basic method, the necessary information is provided within the actual cipher that will be received. The cipher in this case is:

> s t l N N, d n s t l e l i e c c y g t t s d o t s l f s e F x s, U o d W I l M a t l k, e h r f T c
> e s l o T W O r a p A n c a n o o n I l A a o I b t E u o t p i i a h i d w o n f o a k

In Morland's example, the sender and receiver have decided upon a length of nine letters, the shape of a basic parallelogram (in this case, a perfect square of nine rows and nine columns) with three nulls at the beginning, two nulls to complete the parallelogram, and four nulls at the end. By nulls, he means that the first three letters are not part of the message, nor are the last four letters. The final ninth line of the parallelogram, too, will have two unnecessary letters; in other words, the meaningful letters only extend to the seventh place on that line. This cipher, above, provides some of those instructions in the set of letters at the beginning: s t l N N, d n. These act as a kind of embedded command line. The recipient knows from this that:

- They should discard the first three letters, s t l. This is based on the prior agreement that the cipher will begin with three nulls.
- The next two letters N and N indicate that the row and column length will be nine. They know this because on the Numeric Alphabet, a capital N is a 9.

This then directs them to which line on the large triangular template (Figure 6) they should look to for the decryption order (in this case, 659147283).

- The next letter in the cipher, d, is also instructional. Lower-case d is the number two on the key, so this indicates that there are two nulls at the end of the parallelogram. When the recipient creates the grid, below, they will know that the final two letters in the ninth row are unnecessary.
- The next letter, n, is also instructional. It indicates that there will be four nulls at the end of the cipher – so, the final letters f, o, a, and k, should be discarded.

The recipient must then look to their Clavis Universalis to see that the key for a message divided by nine rows is 6 5 9 1 4 7 2 8 3. This must be written into a grid above the cipher to line up with the nine columns, as in Table 2:

Morland does not explain the next step clearly. The reader must divide the letters left in the cipher (discarding the opening three nulls and command set) into nine groups of nine letters. Those units then correspond with the numbers above (so, 6 above dictates which column group 6, below, will be written from top to bottom):

Group 1: s t l e l i e c c
Group 2: y g t (t) s d o t s l – note: Morland has made a mistake on this line. There should be only one lower-case t for the solution to work.
Group 3: f s e F x s, U o d
Group 4: W i l M a t l k, e
Group 5: h r f T c e s l o
Group 6: T W O r a p A n c
Group 7: a n o o n i l A a
Group 8: o I b t E u o t p
Group 9: i i a h i d w o n
　　　　　(readers must remember that the last two letters, o and n, are nulls).

With the cipher divided into nine units of nine letters, they can then create a grid with their Clavis Universalis (key). The number in the key is the location of that group of letters in the cipher (see Table 3).

Once the cipher letters are distributed in this way, the message emerges. The reader must scan, as would have been agreed upon by the parties, from left to right, descending. The solution therefore is:

Table 2 Number key from the Clavis Universalis in Samuel Morland's (1666) *A New Method of Cryptography*

6	5	9	1	4	7	2	8	3

Table 3 Solution grid for cipher in Samuel Morland's (1666) *A New Method of Cryptography*

6	5	9	1	4	7	2	8	3
T	h	i	s	W	a	y	o	f
W	r	i	t	i	n	g	i	s
O	f	a	l	l	o	t	h	e
r	T	h	e	M	o	s	t	F
a	c	i	l	a	n	d	E	x
p	e	d	i	t	i	o	u	s
A	s	w	e	l	l	t	o	U
n	l	o	c	k	A	s	t	o
c	o	n	c	e	a	l	p	d

This Way of Writing is Of all other The Most Facil and Exped itious As well to Unlock As to conceal. (the last two letters p and d, remember, are nulls)

This way of writing is of all other the most facile and expeditious as well to unlock as to conceal.

Morland then demonstrates how the templates could be used with simple direction changes but still lead to the same solution. His algorithm is easily adaptable – for example, by arranging the units of letters in a different shape, or by reading in a different direction – depending upon the situation. On a striking page printed in color, he shows how the following message could be solved using a shape like a "pentagonum centrale" (see Figure 7). The message is: "State cauti, cras hora decima noctis venient hostes, ut invadant Urbem," or "Stand wary, tomorrow at the tenth hour of the night the enemy will come to attack the city."

If one begins at the top of the pentagon, one sees the letter s, then from left to right, descending, t a t e c a u t i, and so forth. Morland does not proceed further into this example, nor does he provide detailed instructions for the next level of ciphering he demonstrates after this with a very long message, with French as the plaintext language, that requires one to arrange the cipher into thirty-four rows and thirty-four columns. There is no way, he notes, that anyone can decipher that complex message without knowing each instruction set. And even if one figures out or has access to all of the instructions, they still would not know the transposition that was agreed upon by the sender and recipient – the shape and order in which to read, which is not encoded in the cipher and "for which he has in a manner no *Data*" (Morland, 1666, 8).

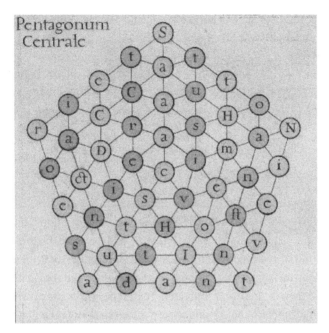

Figure 7 Example of shapes possible for ciphering and deciphering messages in Samuel Morland's (1666) *A New Method of Cryptography.* STC M2781A, page 3, digital image 60226, used by permission of the Folger Shakespeare Library

No correspondence has been found that provides evidence that Morland's *New Method* was adapted for use by Charles II or his court. Certainly, though, Charles II and his correspondents did frequently write in cipher, and their ciphers were complex enough that recipients, like Sir William Temple, needed to struggle with the algorithm. Temple's letters to Charles II provide a clear, and at times amusing, demonstration of his awareness that secret writing demands this new literacy that requires he puzzle through step-by-step. This kind of reading is uncomfortably challenging to him, which he confesses openly. Early in 1668, he expresses his frustration about his failed attempt to understand several lines of a recent letter:

Hague, Feb. 3., N.S. 1668.

My Lord,

I have received two long dispatches from your Lordship of the 18th. by several hands, and except it were about five or six Lines out of Cypher in them, am not one word the Wiser for them both, and know no help in the World for it. If I am such a Dunce, and People will not believe it, all I can say in my defence is, That Sir *Samuel Moorland* was practicing upon me but half hour at most, just before I came away, when my Head was full both of my Dispatches newly ended, and the disposal of my Journey. He promised to send me the Papers and directions before I went, and I to practice them at my leisure. His part was omitted, and thereupon mine was never thought on, since I came away without either Rules or Practice.

(Temple, 1701, 10–11)

Morland promised to provide instructions but apparently never did, so Temple is unable to understand the important message. One can almost imagine Morland's impatient half-hour lesson and his hope that this is enough to get Temple started. His letter emphasizes the factors that can make this kind of reading even more difficult: it requires rest and sharpness which he does not have after the fatigue of traveling, and it also challenges one's confidence in their own intellect. Temple seems wary of what others will think of him for not being able to read the ciphers and take that failure as a mark on his intelligence. In other words, he fears that this exercise materializes and thus makes visible his intellectual shortcomings. In that same letter, he also notes how this kind of reading requires that one operate in an environment with no distractions. He had been engaged with business and interrupted frequently. He is nearly ready to give up ciphering altogether by the end of the letter:

> If this will not serve to excuse my sencelessness in this point, I know not what more to say, unless it be, That God Almighty has given it to other Men to make Cyphers and to flie, but to me only to walk upon plain Ground and to read plain Hands, or plain Cyphers at most. But let my fault be what it will, I am sure I have done Penance enough for it, and spent five or six such Hours about it, that I had rather spend at any time in the Coal Mines, especially ending them without the least success, which is the relief of all Cares and Pains. (Temple, 1701, 10–11)

Temple here emphasizes the amount of time he has invested trying to understand the ciphers. While the instructional manuals promote cryptography as a pleasant and rewarding pursuit, Temple would rather do dirty manual labor. Granted, seventeenth-century works like Wilkins's *Mercury* needed to make the claim that cryptography is easily learnable and entertaining to counter the occult reputation of the discipline; if the everyday reader can master it with minimal training and enjoy doing so, one cannot argue that it is dark magic. Later cryptologists, like Davys, also position cryptography as learnable, yet Davys emphasizes deciphering as an algorithmic process; only those who can work methodically and with the stamina necessary can learn it. Davys notes that he had only recently learned about secret writing from a colleague, Thomas Carte, who was finding ciphered letters in the papers of James Butler, the Duke of Ormond. Carte was writing a book, *Life of the Duke of Ormond* (1736), and had run across a letter to Ormond from Charles I in cipher. Davys notes that "I found it a much easier Task than I expected," so Carte passes several other letters to him to decrypt, which Davys is able to do (Davys, 1737, 1).[28] He is not a genius; he just intuitively works out a series of steps, creating his own method for these relatively easy ciphers.

Despite the complaints, it is a literacy even Temple will develop. Though, in early February 1668, Temple seems to have surrendered to his inability to understand ciphering and deciphering in the way that naturally talented readers like Davys could, by April 3 1668, just two months later, Temple is already confidently exchanging letters that he writes in cipher and that he seems to read easily; at least, he no longer grumbles about it. On April 10, he notes that "I have received your Lordship's of the 23d. past, and perfectly understood all that was written in Cypher, which shews that this has been the first that has come to me exactly written, since to decypher this we went but the ways we try'd in those before" (Temple, 1701, 29). Note here that Temple points to the frequency of error in the writing of cipher, which certainly slows down the decryption process. Even Morland, I noted, made an error in his example. It was certainly common for the ciphers in daily secret writings to have mistakes; sometimes these did not impact the decryption, but they certainly slowed it down. One of Morland's goals in *New Method* is to decrease this possibility by emphasizing the need for strict rules. Algorithmic reading is, perhaps above all else, an attempt to reduce error. In fact, though he adds a lower-case t to his cipher, following the instruction set eventually reveals that this is an error. If there are two nulls designated for the end of the final row, for example, the total number of characters must be seventy-nine to fit in a nine by nine parallelogram (81–2); the extra t makes the remaining cipher eighty characters long, however. The decipherer may not know which letter is mistakenly included, so experimenting with the line groupings to locate it will slow down the process.

The letters between Charles II and Temple do not appear to have used any of these "new" methods by Morland in this court publication, and Temple clearly struggled with a much simpler substitution method. Certainly, there were easier options for writers and readers like Temple. Falconer's *Cryptomenysis*, for example, provides methods that are more in line with the energy that readers like Temple may have wanted to put into ciphering and deciphering.

---

[28] These ciphered letters are today housed in the Bodleian Library in the Carte Papers.

Cryptomenysis demonstrates, perhaps more than any other instructional text, that the algorithmic literacy required in secret writing is diverse and inventive. In this example, Falconer demonstrates how correspondents can choose a simple three-digit number, in this case 436, and agree upon the letters included in the alphabet (abcdefghiklmnopqrstuwxyz). This is all that is needed to create a cipher that is difficult to break without access to the key. If one takes the following plaintext message, they then line up each letter with the number 436 repeated until the end (see also Video 2 for demonstration):

To create the cipher, the writer must take the first letter, T, and beginning the count *with* T, go forward a total of four letters in the alphabet – so, T, U, W, X. The T will then become an x in the cipher. One then counts three letters forward for the second letter in the message, h, again remembering to count h in that step, to arrive at the letter k. One should count forward by six letters, then, for the third letter in the message, e, to again arrive at k. The cipher is thus:

> xkk kqahtsrt ti wnb eoxa dkbqsg etutasworp yr wndw bh ofb etqeqyfk xkkug
> ow ptxkoqi ti dxmdkulk zlqo ukuxk xkk xxxq. (Falconer, 1685, 31)

Because he may be writing in political allegiance to King James II, Falconer's main concern in *Cryptomenysis* is functionality. As Temple's correspondence shows, one needs to actually be able to quickly write and read a cipher in order for it to be useful. The method Falconer shares is easy if one has the key, 436, a short three-number combination to remember, and they know what letters to include in the alphabet. The intended reader need only count backward by four, three, and six for each letter in the sequence. The trickiest part is remembering that the given letter is part of the count.

2.3 Secret Writing and Discernment: Cryptographic Categories

Sissela Bok argues that secrecy is defined by concealment and hiding yet notes that in its Latin roots, *secretum* and *secernere*, a secret is something set apart or separated from, in the sense of a kind of filtering or distinction of parts (Bok, 1984, 6). Mark Neocleous also notes that *secerno* is to separate, set apart, or divide up, similar to a hole in a grain separator that allows the good to pass through while the bad is filtered out (Neocleous, 2002, 90). "It bespeaks discernment," Bok writes, "the ability to make distinctions, to sort out and draw lines: a capacity that underlies not only secrecy but all thinking, all intention and choice" (Bok, 1984, 6). Bok does not follow up with this fascinating thread, instead turning to focus on other terms connected to secrecy, like privacy, silence, stealth, and deceit. The concept of discernment, however, is

Cryptomenyſis Pateſacta :

Or the

A R T

O F

SECRET INFORMATION

Diſcloſed without a *KEY.*

Containing,

Plain and Demonſtrative Rules,

for Decyphering all Manner of S E C R E T
W R I T I N G. With Exact Methods, for Reſol-
ving Secret Intimations by S I G N S or G E-
S T U R E S, or in S P E E C H. As alſo an In-
quiry into the Secret ways of C O N V E Y I N G
Written Meſſages : And the ſeveral M Y S T E-
R I O U S P R O P O S A L S for Secret Informa-
tion, mentioned by *Trithemius,* &c.

By *J. F.*

Et varias uſus meditando extunderet Artes.
Virg. G. i.

L O N D O N,

Printed for *Daniel Brown,* at the black *Swan* and
Bible, without *Temple-Bar,* 1685.

Video 2 Demonstration of encryption of a secret message in John Falconer's
(1685) *Cryptomenysis Patefacta*. Images courtesy of the National Cryptologic
Museum. Video available at www.cambridge.org/secretwriting

helpful as a way of thinking about secret writing and reading processes during
the eighteenth century and is central to algorithmic thinking; ways of making
distinctions, through sorting, categorizing, assembling, disassembling, and

Table 4 Plaintext message in which the key of 436 repeated will be used in decryption in John Falconer's (1685) *Cryptomenysis Patefacta*

4	3	6	4	3	6	4	3	6	4	3	6	4	3	6	4	3	6	4	3	6	4	3	6	4	3	6	4
T	h	e	G	o	v	e	r	n	o	r	o	f	t	h	e	C	i	t	y	i	s	b	e	y	o	n	d

3	6	4	3	6	4	3	6	4	3	6	4	3	6	4	3	6	4	3	6	4	3	6	4	3	6
C	o	r	r	u	p	t	i	o	n	,	s	o	t	h	a	t	w	e	m	a	y	c	o	n	c	l	u	d	e

4	3	6	4	3	6	4	3	6	4	3	6	4	3	6	4	3	6	4	3	6	4
t	h	e	r	e	i	s	n	o	t	h	i	n	g	o	f	B	r	i	b	e	r	i	e	w	i	l	l

3	6	4	3	6	4	3	6	4
s	e	r	v	e	t	h	e	t	u	r	n	.

Table 5 Key for a cipher in John Falconer's (1685) *Cryptomenysis Patefacta*, page 7

1 2 3 4	1 2 3 4	1 2 3 4	1 2 3 4	1 2 3 4	1 2 3 4
a b c d	e f g h	i k l m	n o p q	r s t u	w x y z
1	2	3	4	5	6

finding patterns are necessary in both encryption and decryption methods, and they come to represent processes that demonstrate reason, even smartness.

Cryptography instruction of the period asks readers to think about human language, whether alphabetic, numeric, or symbolic, as it can be categorized in new ways that yield new meanings, as its parts can be disassembled and then combined to hide secrets. This is already how language worked, of course, but that adaptability became more consciously formulized. In other words, cryptography itself became recognized as an art of creative discernment. As the cryptologists of the long eighteenth century show, the number of ways one can make distinctions, sort the properties of language, and even draw lines to manipulate meaning, is limitless. Falconer is particularly innovative with categorization in *Cryptomenysis*, as the 436 cipher shows. In another example, he demonstrates how a writer can group the alphabet in such a way as to provide a deictic key:

From this arrangement of letters, grouped by six units of four, the writer sends the following cipher:

43, 51, 31, 41, 13, 21, 43, 52, 31, 41, 52, 31, 14, 31, 11, 53, 54, 51, 54, 31, 53, 11, 21, 53, 54, 11, 21, 22, 54, 23, 21.

The solution is simple if the reader knows the rules – the ways in which the alphabet should be divided and grouped – and can recreate the key in Table 5. The first digit in each double-digit number refers to the group number. For the 4 in 43, the reader must go to the fourth set of letters (n, o, p, and q). The 3 in 43 then refers to the number within that group, so p. The first letter in the cipher is thus p. Worked fully through, the plaintext is:

p r i n c e p s i n s i d i a t u r u i t a e t u a e f u g e

Princeps insidiatur vitae tuae fuge.[29]

Falconer notes that this method, with more complexity, was discovered in recent correspondence in Scotland. He also explains that in some secret writings of Athanasius Kircher ("Kircherus"), a German Jesuit scholar, this same method is

---

[29] The prince lies in wait for your life.

used but as points in an "arithmetical figure" (Falconer, 1685, 7).[30] In other words, the numbers 4–3, 5–1, 4–1, and so forth refer to the rise and run of a graph, upon which points indicate the number, which in turn refers to the letter groupings.

The reader who does not have access to these rules can still decipher it, but they must use a separate set of steps. First, they should distinguish the vowels from the consonants, be attentive to double letters, and distinguish the vowels from themselves, careful to think across languages. Falconer reminds readers that in English, single-letter words are only vowels. He suggests that readers begin to map out what they already know about global languages; for example, to keep a list of five-letter words, in English, in which the second and last are the same, like which, known, serve, and so on (Falconer, 1685, 11). This promotion of knowing multiple global languages, and understanding their patterns, grammars, and quirks, is important in cryptography.

James Swaine and Joseph Simms's (1761) *Cryptography: Or a New, Easy, and Compendious System of Short-Hand, Adapted to All the Various Arts, Sciences, and Professions* is also respectful of grammar and attentive to methods of categorization to hide communication. They note that what will make their publication unique is their decision to begin with detailed instruction – an "epitome" – on grammar and its taxonomies, which they feel is necessary knowledge for anyone training in the discipline. *Cryptography* begins at the most basic level, defining nouns and verbs and their types, and then proceeds through the units of language, from the alphabet itself to common letter groupings, syllables, types and categories of words, clauses and sentence types, and punctuation. They also include, as part of their "praxis," an introduction to scientific words. Though its title is *Cryptography*, Swaine and Simms's focus is not really on secret writing but on the subject of their subtitle, shorthand, and their goal is to provide translations of scientific publications as (to their minds) more efficient shorthand versions, for which they provide several examples at the end of their volume (Figure 8). Shorthand will certainly be a popular branch of secret communication in the nineteenth century and as the nature of secretarial work will change in industry. While secrecy is not its publicized goal, it does create in-groups and out-groups based on the degree to which one is educated in the special symbols of shorthand. As Swaine and Simms's instruction demonstrates, the grammar of shorthand may be based on the knowable grammar of one's language, but it still requires much memorization of rules.

---

[30] Kircher published widely on a range of topics, from volcanoes to infectious disease, optics, and music. *Polygraphia nova et universalis ex combinatoria arte directa* (1663) is a detailed work on cryptography, and his *Musurgia universalis* (1650) includes musical ciphers.

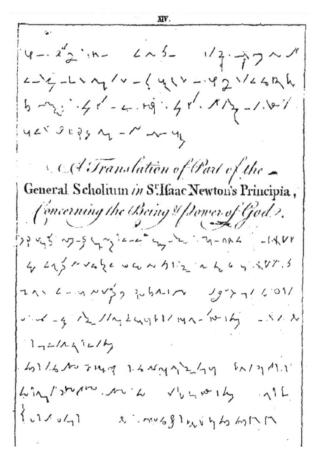

Figure 8 A translation of Isaac Newton's *Principia* into shorthand in James Swaine and Joseph Simms's (1761) *Cryptography: Or a New, Easy, and Compendious System of Short-Hand, Adapted to All the Various Arts, Sciences, and Professions*. Courtesy of the Library of Congress

2.4 Deconstructions of Grammar: Separation and Recombination

As Swain and Simms emphasize, cryptographic training during the eighteenth century requires an excitement for grammar and its taxonomies. And grammar, with all its possible combinations, is central to what it means to be a thinking person. Joshua Oldfield's (1707) *Essay Towards the Improvement of Reason*, similarly, provides a long explication of reason as visibly represented through the cognitive activities of combination, separation, abstraction, relation, and expression. Oldfield theorizes that human beings are inherently combinations – of parts of the body and of material substances, of actions and behaviors, of emotions, of influences, and of accidents and errors (Oldfield, 1707, 61). The world is organized too, he notes, as a series of types of combinations; people gather to become societies, threads weave to become knots and fabrics, nerves and ligaments entwine to become muscles and moving bodies, sand accumulates to become beaches. Language is an act of combination in order to express meaning. Separation is also ontological; sometimes things, people, and other entities must be pulled apart and distinguished. Complex thinking may be more productive when ideas and concepts are separated and analyzed individually, yet with recognition of the ways in which meaning changes in different combinations.

> The living Body, that has now its Arms and Legs, may be conceiv'd as if it were actually without them. These two Sorts may be term'd in some sense Mental-Separations, but especially the latter: We proceed to what is Real in one way or other, and
> S 14. (3) There may be in the same intire Body a lineal Separation, as by a Line drawn on Paper, or the Appearance of a Crack in firm and solid Marble. (4) We may take up only some part of what lay together, in a Tho't, a Sentence, a Book, an House, an Age, or in the World, to be the subject of our Consideration and Discourse. (Oldfield, 1707, 64)

Secret communication instruction engages with this celebration of combination, separation, abstraction, relation, and expression more obviously than other language training of the period. Charles La Fin's (1692) *Sermo Mirabilis: or the Silent Language*), for example, is perhaps most explicit about the importance of combinatory discernment. It is specifically about sending secret messages *through* parts of the body, through what we would today call sign language. La Fin explains how he had once warned a friend that a sergeant was coming to arrest him by gesturing from across a tavern. He notes how another man courted a daughter, expressing his love in signs, while the father was sitting in the same room. This secret gesturing is effective because the tendency of human observation is to take in scenes as a whole without great attention to the parts or the peripheries. Further, this form of bodily ciphering is easier to learn than cryptography. "One may learn perfectly in the space of six hours," he notes, "how to impart his mind to his Friend in any Language, *English, Latin, French, Dutch &c.*, tho never so deep and dangerous a Secret, without the least Noise, Word or Voice; and without the Knowledge of any in Company" (La Fin, 1692, title page).

Thicknesse also emphasizes methods of separation and recombination in real-world ciphering and deciphering, which he, too, promotes as a means of self-improvement in *A Treatise on the Art of Decyphering and of Writing in Cypher.* His own methods are so learnable, he notes, that "a Man of good sense, who has never considered the Matter attentively, will at first think very difficult; but in a few hours consideration, be as much surprised as pleased, at the unfolding of this seemingly occult Art" (Thicknesse, 1772, viii–ix). He has clearly read

Falconer as well as Wilkins and Bacon. To Falconer's easy methods, Thicknesse prefers the biliteral cipher that Bacon explained (but did not invent) as well as Wilkins's "biharmonic" cipher in *Mercury*. This cipher, as well as Thicknesse's improvement upon it, is explained in Section 3 of this Element.

2.5 Reading As Deciphering: Simultaneity and Pattern Recognition

As evidenced by Temple's reluctant acknowledgment that reading ciphers is a necessary skill for the modern politician, by the late seventeenth and eighteenth centuries, deciphering came into vogue. Falconer, Thicknesse, and Davys helped shift the conversation about privacy and self-protection toward the need for new methods of reading. These reading processes were, and still are, largely inductive in nature. Faced with new ciphers, decipherers work first from a series of observations, looking for patterns, and then begin to make assumptions about the cipher's language, genre, writer, location, and content. This is why Davys notes that the language of "guessing" is more fitting for deciphering than scientific and mathematic terms. And as in inductive reasoning, the conclusion is not necessarily fully correct. There might be errors and missing pieces, but the goal is for enough content to be identified that the reader can take action. If the induction leads the reader to identify the rules by which the cipher was constructed, they can then work backward, deductively, to double check the work. During the decryption, the reader must *think* as the writer, must consider the reading simultaneously with the writing, imagining the writer's process. One of More's (1716) lessons on penmanship in *Of the First Invention of Writing* provides a sense of how this simultaneity of reading and writing works in decryption, though he is not walking readers through a cipher. More provides readers with a very faint, chalky set of lines surrounded by ornamentation and faces. The task for the reader is to recreate the writing by filling in the blanks, through a process of close reading.

In the process of struggling to make out More's words in this exercise, readers are simulating the original writer's physical act of composition, as Jonathan Goldberg notes is common in instructional writing texts. Robin E. Rider finds that this step-by-step problem solving via reenactment, with simultaneous reading and copying, becomes common in eighteenth-century instruction in algebra as well: "To make sense of a series of algebraic derivations, readers, whether novices or the unconvinced, were urged to retrace those steps by writing them out themselves, recapitulating with a pen the author's progress, line by line, from initial conditions to final result" (Goldberg, 2020, 473).[31]

---

[31] See also Roger Chartier 's discussion of copying script in print manuals in *The Author's Hand and the Printer's Mind*. Translated by Lydia G. Cochrane (Cambridge: Cambridge University Press, 2014). See also Adrian Johns, *The Nature of the Book: Print and Knowledge in the Making* (Chicago: The University of Chicago Press, 1998).

More's exercise does not only require the student of penmanship to copy the passage perfectly, however: it invites the reader to diverge from the template. Though very difficult to read, it says:

> Contrive each little Turn, Mark every Space
> The Painters first chalk out the intended Face;
> Yet be not fondly your own slave for this
> But change hereafter what appears amiss.

The passage emphasizes the reader's close scrutiny of the text as they navigate it as a writer and stresses the inductive process it requires, but the message itself emphasizes flexibility and adaptability, that the lesson is as much about learning how to adjust for error on the spot than about meticulous penmanship.

It is interesting to note that More's verse, here, is not original. It is itself a copy, just as it is also asking readers to copy the image with their pens. The lines are common in writing manuals with slight variations, but originally it appears to come from a much longer poem, John Sheffield's (1682) *An Essay upon Poetry*.[32] These four lines in Sheffield's poem are not about writing skills, in the same sense as More's, or about penmanship. With a variation of "intended face" as "future face" in Sheffield's original, Sheffield is explaining how difficult it is for playwrights to write dialogue. He emphasizes that they should be inspired by Shakepeare, Marlowe, and other great playwrights in their construction of character and speech, but they must not strive to create perfection – no human being is perfect in reality, and the dialogue and the characters' faults must drive the plot. These lines are followed by this couplet in Sheffield's version: "Think not so much where shining thoughts to place/As what a man would say in such a case" (Sheffield, 1682, 15). Sheffield's verse is about authenticity in fiction and the power of writing to capture character. It is interesting, then, that this is the moment More copies for his lesson; in a sense, he is showing that adaptability (literally) that his message promotes. Sheffield's message that readers must not miss the more important big picture in pursuit of perfection in details, too, aligns with More's approach to writing as a material manifestation of intelligence.

Thicknesse stresses that he is not an expert or an innovator but that he is capable of "leading those who doubt it"; importantly, he argues that deciphering is a "rational Exercise for the mind" – it is a habit of thinking that is beneficial to all readers (and especially young people, he notes), even if they do not have any real purpose for deciphering in their daily lives (Thicknesse, 1772, ix). The appeal of deciphering by the late eighteenth century is that it provides a "methodical Way of

---

[32] Thank you to Holly Faith Nelson for assistance interpreting the word "slave" and for identifying earlier usage in Sheffield's poem.

thinking, on any one Subject" (Thicknesse, 1772, ix). The mind that is trained in rational, step-by-step thinking when young, he emphasizes, becomes a stronger mind when aged. Thicknesse's work is different from the seventeenth-century instruction, though, in his interest in the habitual mistakes that amateur cipherers make, which a decipherer must be aware of.[33] For example, he notes that when using a substitution method using arbitrary characters (marks that might look like shorthand symbols, for instance), which is relatively simple, inexperienced writers will begin with A and choose easy characters, but as they proceed through the rest of the alphabet, the characters will become more elaborate. A decipherer who knows this tendency can already, then, begin to categorize the characters by where they likely go in the alphabet. So, before one even begins considering the grammar of a message, they must consider what is predictable about human behavior – that writers become fatigued, more elaborate, and more prone to error over time. This growing interest in how writing reflects the interiority of the author is present in other writing instruction of the later eighteenth century as well, as Aileen Douglas points out convincingly. Douglas finds that by the early nineteenth century, exercises in script, embedded within the print manuals, are less about discipline and increasingly "associated with agency and personal autonomy" (Douglas, 2017, 19).

Intimate knowledge of grammar and the eccentricities of global languages are fundamental in deciphering. In fact, awareness of the spelling and grammatical patterns of many languages makes deciphering a much easier task than most assume. Thicknesse notes that words with double letters, like "eel" and "look" are first clues, as are words that are symmetrical, like "did" (Thicknesse, 1772, 23). Knowledge of where vowels and consonants tend to appear, and of what consonants are typically paired, is common. In general, then, Thicknesse advocates for readers to realize that they know much more about language than they think they do, that there are patterns they have always observed and internalized that they simply need to recognize as sources of knowledge. Frequency analysis, too, is a natural ability, he notes. One can easily deduce which letters are most common in their language, and in other languages they cannot even read; similar predictions are also intuitive, such as knowing which words often appear together in common phrases (Thicknesse, 1772, 25). Thicknesse notes one experience reading a message that a friend thought would be impossible. The cipher was in Ethiopian and Etruscan alphabets, though the maintext was in French and English (Thicknesse, 1772, 90–94). Even with these linguistic layers, he is able to solve it quickly because of his basic understanding of grammar (nouns, verbs, propositions, articles, repetitions, etc.).

---

[33] It is perhaps ironic that his own text contains so many errors.

In "The Art of Decyphering Discovered," the poet writes about the ways in which cryptographers notice patterns in language that they did not realize they know:

> In vain to puzzle you they try,
> Who deal in odd Cryptography;
> Who *This* for *That* at Pleasure set,
> And forming new the Alphabet,
> Contiguous Words together blend,
> Without Beginning, without End.
>   (Anonymous, 1727, 4)

In these lines, the poet is noting that a good cryptographer will exploit the reader's expectations, aware of conventions and the cognitive dissonance it causes when they are disrupted. They form new alphabets, and they run words together in ways that confuse their reading. In a good cipher, a reader does not know where to begin and where to end – unless they have trained in algorithmic thinking and come to the cipher with a set of methods and steps. The woman who receives the cipher in this poem has received at least some training, so those who "deal" in cryptography may work "in vain" to trick her.

The poet also emphasizes the conscious process of discernment that the lady must then engage in to solve the cipher, in this case recognizing the patterns she knows exist in the English language:

> The Vowels first become your Prey,
> Themselves conspiring to betray;
> And prove less formidable far,
> By how much more their Numbers are.
> The bulky Consonant succeeds
> Next Object of your martial Deeds;
> While you with proper Arms salute,
> The gentle *Liquid* and rough *Mute*,
> Whose Fate so early is not fix'd,
> When interchangeably they're mix'd;
> But a short date of Life is theirs,
> If they presume to march by Pairs.
>   (Anonymous, 1727, 5)

Disassemblage, combination, and recombination are compositional not only on the level of alphabetic or numeric characters. The materialities of the instruments and surfaces themselves – whether paper, flesh, stone, air – can also be manipulated. The lady must here engage physically with a moving, changing text, and the "liquid" of the ink is itself an active agent in the message's meaning. Through broad graphic writing practices, cryptologists leveraged print and other communication technologies of their generation, like special inks, papers, and the post, to preserve privacy.

3 Cipher Devices As Writing and Reading Technologies

Secret writing requires – and inspires – several types of technological intervention and support. Section 2 examined the ways in which alphabets, numbers, words, and grammars were manipulated to obscure and reveal meaning as unique writing and reading processes. There were also technologies of the material act of writing that allowed obscurity, like precision instruments, disappearing inks, and writing surfaces that could be transformed to hide and reveal. Every surface was graphically malleable. Rock, wood, flesh, paper, and cloth were familiar fields, but they could also be maneuvered to become communicative in unobvious ways. As Thicknesse reminds the reader, communication by writing always involves an act of physical transportation that makes a message vulnerable. If a messenger or postal delivery person is murdered and their packages stolen, the writing must resist disclosure (Thicknese, 1772, 12). Secret writing also invites new technologies of reading, for which Morland provides some creative examples. There are supportive optical and aural devices, such as glasses and listening trumpets for magnification and clarity, as well as computing tools that assist the mind during the calculation and processing stages. In addition, there are also storage and retrieval technologies that are necessary for secret communication. Alan Stewart explains the importance of the closet, for example, as a space that facilitates secrecy, and closets, especially as secretarial offices, also include technologies like cabinets and filing systems.

As I argue in *A Material History of Medieval and Early Modern Ciphers* (Ellison, 2017), secret writing technologies were, perhaps ironically, technologies of *connection* above all else. They attempted to make visible and traceable the cognitive processes at work in calculation and problem solving and to share those processes with others, even nonexperts or amateur mathematicians. Thicknesse begins his *Treatise* on ciphering with a fitting technological comparison between secret writing and the invention of glass windows:

> We have Windows and Glass Doors which let in the Air, and the Light, at the same Time that they shut out, the Injuries and Inconveniences which attend them, and exhibit to us, even in the interior Parts of our House, the variegated View of Nature, which transform the Winds, the Frosts, and the Tempests, into a magnificent moving Picture before our Eyes. (Thicknesse, 1772, iv)

At the same time that it offers protection and privacy, glass also allows one to stay better engaged with the outside world. It allows an interiority that is also fully visible. Ciphering, too, provides security from threats and injury, and though it would seem to be an invention for closed communication, it is positioned by cryptologists as encouraging fuller, more open conversation, but with (allegedly, ideally) safe boundaries. And like glass, for Thicknesse, it is at once a barrier and a transparency. Further, Thicknesse suggests that glass provides the lower classes with comfort, with the implication that secret writing does as well: "The Peasant, in these our Days, is thought miserable, who wants a Luxury which a *Roman* Emperor was a Stranger to!" One of the promises of early cryptography is that the technological creativity that secret writing inspires is a benefit to all, not just politicians, the military, and aristocrats.

3.1 Writing Instruments

Certainly, writing instruction had already been interested in technologies that allowed greater precision, speed, and versatility. What counted as writing "instruments" was broad and creative; pens themselves could be of many types, and other kinds of instruments were also common, like knives, rocks, and even parts of the body. Cryptographic practices well before the long eighteenth century, too, were clearly technologically savvy about writing instrumentation. Lighting fires in towers to signal approaching armies, or using smoke to pass messages quickly across terrains, were common across world cultures. Thicknesse mentions that these methods are used often during the eighteenth century, such as by the Spanish military regime stationed near Gibraltar during the War of the Spanish Succession in 1702. They used fires to report on the ships in the bay to the Governor of Cádiz (Thicknesse, 1772, 31). If only the British General William Hargrave had known this, he could have interrupted the communication quite easily by lighting his own fires in strategic places to confuse the message. Thicknesse claims that the Spanish still use this same method at that location, and that he alone has discovered it. Yet, he fears a court-martial should he expose the shortcomings of British military officials. He publishes it in the *Treatise* because he feels he is at a safe distance.

Pens and their inks are also a source of great potential for cryptologists. Thicknesse describes dipping a pen in a solution of sal ammoniac and water so that secret writing is not visible until held up to a fire or light.[34] This is a poor, temporary method, however, as the acid will corrode quickly and reveal the message. He prefers dissolved alum, which requires that a paper be dipped in water. He notes, too, that "letters written with urine, goat's fat, or hog's lard, will not appear 'till dust is thrown upon them; and it was by this stratagem, that *Attelus* obtained a victory over the *Gauls*" (Thicknesse, 1772, 96). One can also write in egg yolk, then black out the paper with ink; the recipient must scrape the paper with a knife, and the areas written in egg yolk will come off (Thicknesse, 1772, 97).

---

[34] Sal ammoniac is a natural mineralogic form of ammonium chloride sometimes harvested from volcanoes. It is water soluble. It has many uses, such as invisible writing, but in the eighteenth century it was also popular as a way of adding intense colors to pyrotechnics. See John A. Conkling and Christopher J. Mocella's *Chemistry of Pyrotechnics* (2010).

He is interested, too, in a method he cites from the German Jesuit and scientist Gaspard Schott (P. Gasparis Schotti, who published *Schola steganographica* in 1665), of using two inks, one diluted with water so that it is very faint, for the real message, the other an ink mixed with beaten gunpowder mixed with rain water to write over top of the secret message. When the recipient dips a sponge in galls and rubs it across the paper, the gunpowder will wash off while the diluted regular ink will darken.

Cryptography inspired new and advanced technologies, but it was also a discipline to which those invested in older types of hand-made artistry looked to preserve their crafts. John Wilkes's *The Art of Making Pens Scientifically* (ca. 1799), which contains a section on *Directions for Secret Writing*, illustrates this connection. This brief booklet is primarily a rhetorical defense of penmaking as a profession and as an art, a reaction against industrialism and the apparently new trend of using machines to produce identical pens and the death, Wilkes fears, of long-lasting homemade inks. He notes that printing relies upon ink that cannot last as long, thus documents will not survive as they once had. These industrialized pens and inks, he laments, are poor quality, not made with mathematical precision, and lack the character of custom pens. With little transition from a lengthy explication of the methods for making superior pens and ink, Wilkes writes, "It may not now be improper to say something of Secret Writing, and the manner of doing it, on which Bishop Wilkins, in his book Mathematical Magic, speaks largely; but it is principally concerning writing in cypher, which requires great pains, and an uncommon share of ingenuity, both in writers and readers" (Wilkes, 1799, 52). Wilkes's main interests are in invisible inks and in clever methods of communicating secrets by manipulating paper. For example, readers can learn to cut a series of randomly spaced boxed-shaped holes in a sheet of paper, place that on another sheet, and write the words of the intended message in those boxes. Then, removing the top sheet with holes, fill in the rest of the space in the bottom paper with random words to create a false message that is unintelligible. The recipient would be sent the "key" (the paper with the boxed holes) separately, to place over the confusing letter to reveal the message. This, and his other examples, are not particularly innovative methods, but Wilkes's choice to include this brief section reveals that still, by the turn of the nineteenth century, secret writing maintains its connection to the technology of the pen.

The human body can be used in other ways as an instrument of secret writing, beyond holding a pen or carving knife. Morland innovates what he calls a *Digital Index*, which is a small thimble with a pointed end that can be inserted in the holes of his Machina Cyclologica Cryptographica, described in this section. This prosthetic is worn on the third finger of the right hand and allows the reader to switch quickly between writing and spinning the dial of the cipher wheel to locate the correct letters or numbers without setting down the pen. The speed and multitasking of writing that is facilitated by this index is unique across the instructional texts. The idea of being able to "turn on and off" the foramen, or the holes that select or deselect the letters, is also novel.

In *Writing Matter*, Goldberg discusses the violence inherent in instruments of writing during the early modern period; for example, the knife that sharpens and molds the quill, the quill that cuts into the page, and the hand that grips the quill as weapon. "The emergence of the writer can be read through these scenes of violence," Goldberg notes, "as the tools of the trade are made ready, as the knife is wielded to produce the pen" (Goldberg, 1990, 80). As Christina Lupton discusses, too, "sixteenth-century writing manuals pictured knives and pens as part of a pedagogical formation in which the hand of the subject is severed from his body and then re-educated as an instrument under his control" (Lupton, 2014, 608). That body becomes dead, in a sense, as the hand takes power; rigorous, frequent penmanship practice renders the hand automatic. Yet, during the eighteenth century, Lupton finds, fictional it-narratives reanimate the bodies that control the pens, and the pens themselves come to life as well as the surviving remnants of living beings, like geese and ostriches. The pens mediate a traumatic relationship between the animal and the human. We see this reanimation of the body in cryptology, too. The instrument that ciphers and deciphers secrets is not disembodied, as Goldberg finds, but intimately and cognitively one with the body that controls it; cryptography is a fully physical experience involving the hands, the eyes, the ears, the mouth, and every part of a person, all working with the mind to hide or disclose important information. Morland's *Digital Index* even requires that the instrument *becomes* a prosthetic. There is, certainly, potential violence in this physicality, but the goal is also to avoid violence, to save the body from threat.

3.2 Writing Surfaces

The anecdote that is repeated most frequently in early ciphering instruction, about the slave who delivers a basket of goods that he consumes along the way, only to be "caught" by the paper invoice that accompanies him, demonstrates the importance of the writing surface for cryptographers. Also popular is the story of the slave on whose flesh a secret message was scarified by the tyrant *Histiaeus*. After enough hair was grown to conceal it, the slave was sent to deliver goods, with the request upon arrival that his head be shaved. It was important that the slave not know that a message was inscribed upon his skin so that "the messenger's head delivered a secret which never troubled his brain" (Thicknesse, 1772, 101). Though *Histiaeus's* goal is that the subject carries the secret unknowingly, what one writes upon is not passive, blank, inanimate, or powerless. Its materiality is as important as the message it carries. Not only is it transportable and malleable in different kinds of ways depending upon the material, it can also keep its message temporarily or permanently. It is also, often, recyclable. It is also, often, living. The slave's "brain," even in this example, *is* no doubt troubled, as he is required to physically travel to enemy territory and risk his safety as unwilling text.

Living and deceased bodies can operate as some of the most effective writing surfaces. Tattoos and scarification are common means of putting messages into motion. Animals can be used both as carriers and as surfaces. Merchants could stuff secret messages into specimen from exotic locations before they were transported to England and Europe for display in fashionable wealthy households or with collectors. Notes could be written on the underside of a dog's collar, too, or gently written onto the flesh of an inflated and then deflated animal bladder. Eggs were commonly used in a variety of ways. The yolk and white could be used to write with, the eggshell could be written upon, or the shell could be delicately opened and then sealed back shut to hide a message stored inside. Communication could be hidden on a deceased human body or inside a pile of the dead, too; few cared to search through those kinds of writing surfaces, especially when bodies were badly damaged or diseased.

Everyday objects, too, are effective as texts. Thicknesse describes using the scabbards of a sword, baked paste inside of bread, and a candle upon which a letter is wrapped around its lower half, then dipped again in hot wax to hide it "to light him to his business" (Thicknesse, 1772, 100). Not only small, easily ignored objects can be surfaces; landscapes that one takes in with their full peripheral vision can also be manipulated to cheat the eye in interesting ways. Walking down a street in town, for example, one might notice that there are ciphers posted on the doors and shutters of a besieged town. One must look around the street as if it is a text, reading from one direction to the other, to see the symbols or letters that, combined, tell a story (Thicknesse, 1772, 95). Gustavus Selenus provides an example of this type of visual ciphering in a final examination for the student of his instructional text, *Cryptomenytices et cryptographiae libri IX* (Selenus, 1624), which I walk through in Section 4. It is a multimodal cipher, in this case expressed as an illustration that might appear in a book or in an artwork, but the idea is applicable in the three-dimensional space of an everyday landscape as well (see Figure 23).

Thicknesse is fascinated by a method in which two staffs, or staves, are provided to the sender and receiver. They have shared instruction on where to attach a piece of parchment that is then wrapped around the staff "in a serpentine revolution" so that its ends line up in such a way that it reveals a message

(Thicknesse, 1772, 18). Without this particular wrapping technique, the parchment's surface will feature scattered pieces of letters. In another method, a piece of paper is twisted to make a spiral tube out of itself in which letters align. The recipient would need to know only what the circumference of the tube must be. Thicknesse also suggests that a reader consider rolling a message into a scroll and then cutting it down the middle between words or letters to create the appearance of two messages. Falconer had already demonstrated a similar idea in an example that involves folding (see Video 3).

In the letter in *Cryptomenysis* in Figure 9, for example, the sender appears to tell the recipient that all is well. If the reader looks closely, they can see a faint white line where the words and letters in each line are separated by a small gap (between "not in," "no thing," "flight we," "me by," "hence, I," etc.). To see the line more easily, one can tilt the message so that the eye looks horizontally across the plane of the epistle. Fold the message along this line, and the real message is revealed in Figure 10.

The epistle was of course a most common genre for secret communication, and cryptographers seized on the ways in which handwriting could be exploited, as I discuss further in Section 4. This kind of double writing – a full letter that appears to say one thing but can be folded to reveal the opposite intent – is not too practical in emergency situations given how much time it might take to write it. Yet, it demonstrates the ways in which cryptologists pushed the limits of their media.

Print technology was also, perhaps surprisingly, a playground of possibilities for cryptographers. Not only were they printing their instructional manuals and being typographically creative, which Section 4 will explore, but they were also using print in interesting ways in the ciphering and deciphering processes. Morland

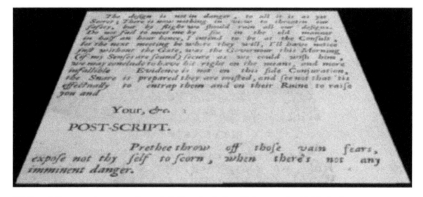

Video 3 Letter that requires folding in John Falconer's (1685) *Cryptomenysis Patefacta*. Images courtesy of the National Cryptologic Museum. Video available at www.cambridge.org/secretwriting

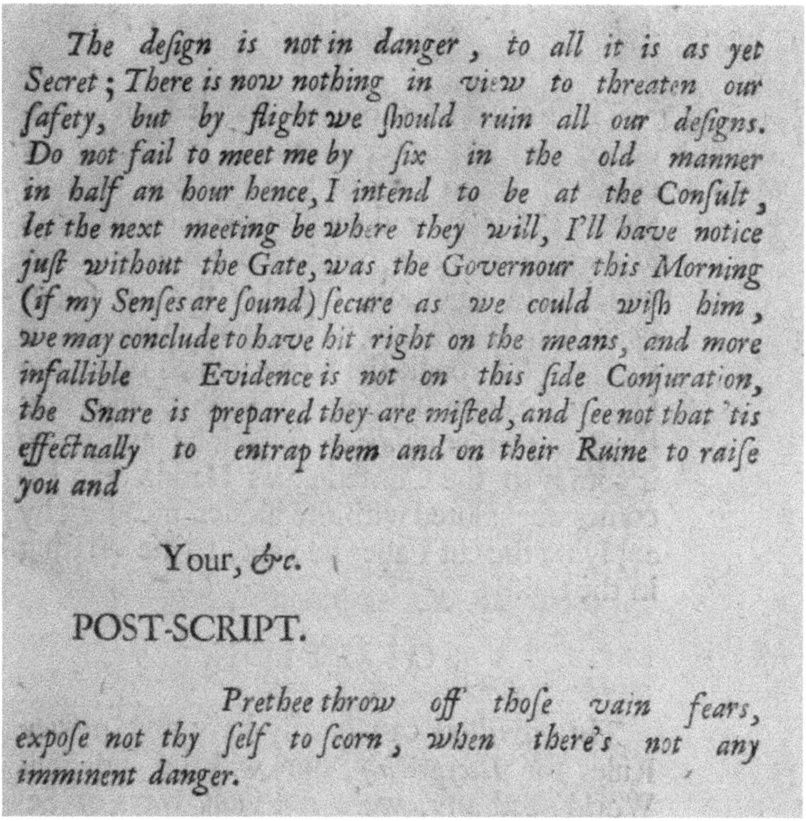

The defign is not in danger, to all it is as yet Secret; There is now nothing in view to threaten our fafety, but by flight we fhould ruin all our defigns. Do not fail to meet me by fix in the old manner in half an hour hence, I intend to be at the Confult, let the next meeting be where they will, I'll have notice juft without the Gate, was the Governour this Morning (if my Senfes are found) fecure as we could wifh him, we may conclude to have hit right on the means, and more infallible Evidence is not on this fide Conjuration, the Snare is prepared they are mifted, and fee not that 'tis effectually to entrap them and on their Ruine to raife you and

Your, &c.

POST-SCRIPT.

Prethee throw off thofe vain fears, expofe not thy felf to fcorn, when there's not any imminent danger.

Figure 9 Example secret letter in John Falconer's (1685) *Cryptomenysis Patefacta*. Courtesy of the National Cryptologic Museum

suggests that correspondents print a collection of templates so that they can quickly enter the data they need to speed the solution process. Those templates, then, are interactive; not only are they meant to be written on by hand as a worksheet, they can also be torn, cut into pieces to be moved around, pricked to create holes for aligning layers, and folded. Punctures could also serve as entry and exit points for weaving string (through paper, wood, bone, or other surfaces as well) to connect alphabetic characters and numbers. Printing in color offered a range of other quick options as well. The replicability of print – yet also its inability to make every copy *completely* identical – was also useful. The slightest variations in a print copy – like the omission of a single ornament in a decorative heading or border, for example – could communicate meaning. Morland was interested, too, in technologies of copying. In the central London Post Office, he was known for a machine that transcribed personal letters in the handwriting of the correspondents; this way, he could keep the copies while the originals were sent on, avoiding delay of delivery

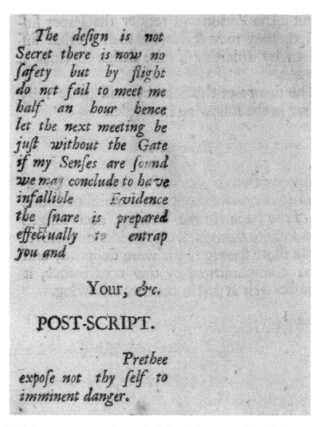

The *defign* is *not* Secret there is *now* no *fafety* but by *flight* do not fail to meet me half an hour hence let the next meeting be *juft* *without* the Gate if my *Senfes* are *found* we may conclude to have *infallible* Evidence the *fnare* is prepared *effectually* to entrap you and

Your, &c.

POST-SCRIPT.

Prethee expofe not thy felf to imminent danger.

Figure 10 Solution to secret letter in John Falconer's (1685) *Cryptomenysis Patefacta*. Courtesy of the National Cryptologic Museum

and suspicion. The copies could then be analyzed for ciphers. A. Buonafalce refers to this as Morland's double-writing machine.

3.3 Reading Devices

The long eighteenth century witnessed the development of early word process-ing tools to (attempt to) increase the efficiency and accuracy of ciphering and deciphering. These devices, including cipher disks of varying complexity, calculation machines and early computers, slide rules, and organizational cab-inets, further demonstrate how cryptography contributed to changes in writing and reading processes. Mechanical devices in cryptography were certainly described in pre-early modern instructional texts. Cryptographers had long sought efficient technical means of speeding the ciphering and deciphering processes for urgent situations. The staffs that Thicknesse mention have histor-ical precedence, for example. Greek priests had used a "Kontakion," or

"*Contacium*," which is a short staff around which are wound many long strips of paper with writings. These could easily be adapted for secret communication.

Late seventeenth- and eighteenth-century cryptologists were continuously inspired by the mechanical creativity of Johannes Trithemius, who included fascinating paper machines within the pages of *Polygraphiae libri sex* (1518) (see Figure 11).[35] While Trithemius's mysterious ciphers have been the subject of many publications – and were conclusively solved in 1996 and 1998 – little attention has been given to the small devices enclosed within his texts. These are part of the book's pages and are fully functional (apparently with a kind of substance or glue that allows wheels to rotate in a full 360 degrees), transforming the book itself into a machine.

Later cryptologists marveled at the aesthetic and mechanical sophistication of Trithemius's cipher wheels, but they did not have much practical value. Morland's inventions of the late seventeenth century, however, helped pave the way for the imaginative future of computing and government observation. They supported his larger vision of a state surveillance system that deterred citizen immorality, which he outlined in the undated "The Nature and Reason of Intelligence." Morland did not belong to or innovate for the Royal Society, and he does not appear to have worked for a guild. He was a Clerk of the Signet in the Post Office for Oliver Cromwell and Gentleman of the Privy Chamber, which means that he was part of a network of government innovators outside of the Royal Society. He invented mathematical instruments, decryption devices, diving bells, gun carriages, speaking trumpets, water pumps, and steam engines.

In 1666, when *New Method* was printed, Morland was working in the Post Office for Charles II, having shifted political alliances, alongside expert mathematician and decipherer John Wallis. Though Morland had been offered a knighthood and a baronetship for his clandestine service to Charles before his return, he did not receive any substantial income or land for his position. So, he began adding other ventures to his resumé. *New Method* is likely one of those projects, as were the calculating machines that he began producing. *New Method* was published in 1666, but it is not clear if this was before or after the London fire that year, which destroyed the Post Office and, along with it, most of the devices he had invented to unseal and reseal letters and make copies. J. R. Ratcliff notes that in 1663, Morland made a gearwork trigonometrical instrument and in 1666 some devices for addition, subtraction, multiplication, and division. They were made by the Sutton workshop, run by Henry Sutton and Samuel Knibb. This was a well-known workshop for mathematical instruments,

---

[35] Trithemius was a German Benedictine abbot who published on lexicography, the occult, and cryptography. He valued education and built a large library collection at his monastery in Sponheim, Germany.

Figure 11 A working cipher device in Johannes Trithemius's *Polygraphiae libri sex, Ioannis Trithemii abbatis Peapolitani, quondam Spanheimensis, ad Maximilianum Caesarem* (1518). The center circle is raised and attached with a kind of substance that is not viewable; the rectangular ruler then twists around that center circle and can go fully around to line up with the alphabets on each section of the wheel. Courtesy of the National Cryptologic Museum

and Morland's work was still being sold as late as 1710 (Ratcliff, 2007, 164). When Morland leased Vauxhall, he used the property to display his inventions.

As numeracy devices, Morland's instruments were not that innovative. They basically added gears to common calculating tools. Where Morland was savvy – and historically influential – was in his marketing of these memory-aid devices to the fashionable public. On his addition machine, he promoted his own name on the surface, as inventor, which was uncommon. He was also strategically targeted in his design: he focused more on the user interface, for instance, than some other mechanics. While Charles Cotterell's mathematical devices were made of cheap materials, Morland had firms produce his in gilt, silver-plated brass, luxurious woods, and crystal. He understood that the user's tactile experience and physical interaction with the device could be *pleasurable*. He worked to make gears smoother than usual, to fit the devices to the human hand and in portable sizes to sit snugly in pockets, to emphasize the digital as well as visual sensation of use. His instruments were fashion accessories. For the Medici family in Italy, he even designed an original calculator with an oddly ornate shape.[36] His stylized choices earned him criticism by Samuel Pepys during a dinner, who said his devices were "pretty but not very useful" (Pepys, 2000, 115).[37] Despite Pepys's opinion, others at that meal had not only heard about Morland's instruments but had also purchased one. He was therefore a pioneer in digitization, creating a new market for devices that are hand held, touch screen, and portable.

In one sense, Morland's machines might more accurately be called anti-writing machines. They were designed to allow the user to avoid writing down numbers or alphabets, to substitute a new technology of memory for writing. His Machina Cyclological Trigonometrica, for example, was a drawing instrument that reached solutions without needing pen or paper (Ratcliff, 2007, 168). Yet, Morland also imitated pen-to-paper mathematics more than other inventors. That his machines do not have the carry function, for example, is a weakness, yet it also points to their closeness to manual paper solution. His Machina Cyclologica Cryptographica (Figure 12) includes the prosthetic stylus I mentioned in Section 2, so the user must still "write" in the sense that they must manipulate the interface by hand, with a pen-like instrument – not everything was automated. Further, the complexity of the machines – Morland's but also those of other inventors – meant that instructions were necessary.

Morland's *New Method* includes pages describing and illustrating the Machina Cyclologica Cryptographica, a cipher wheel or cipher disk with multiple layers, allowing users to decipher complex messages more quickly. Including the description and diagram of the Machina Cyclologica

---

[36] Ratcliff speculates about whether the design was hastily created, to appeal to the Medici prince, Cosimo III, or whether he copied an Italian design and adapted it to his calculator (2007, 176–7).

[37] This is the entry from March 14, 1667/1668.

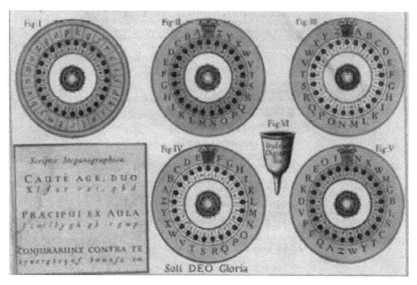

Figure 12 Samuel Morland's (1666) Machina Cyclologica Cryptographica in *New Method of Cryptography*. By permission of the Folger Shakespeare Library. STC M2781A, page 12, digital image 83906

Cryptographica in *New Method* was not informative only; it is a clever advertising strategy to pique Charles II's interest in his new device and its political, as well as fashionable, uses. Though he saw some commercial success, as illustrated by Pepys's dinner party, Charles II and his court (and the courts of other nations) were Morland's main target audience. The instructions are difficult to follow, as were instructions in several of his mechanical publications. Prince Cosimo III of the Medici family, for example, asked Morland repeatedly for clearer written directions to use the gift he had received, the *Maccina Calcolatrice*.

Ratcliff rightfully questions the influence of Morland and his fashionable technologies. What interests me is how they reveal a changing culture of literacy during the late seventeenth century, a culture in which writing and reading processes are openly and increasingly prostheticized and technologically assisted. There is clear experimentation with the idea of the human–computer interface. My argument is that cryptographers helped the public see how writing technologies they had grown accustomed to, like the printed book, had standardized their composition and reading processes to such an extent that they could obscure peripheral vision. These new devices help counter that tunnel vision, in some ways, yet also exaggerate it, in others.

Later eighteenth-century devices seem less interested in changing the culture of writing and reading than Morland's, with less attention to aesthetics and marketability, but they were increasingly functional. The famous wooden cipher cylinder created by Thomas Jefferson in 1795 (called the Jefferson disk or Bazeries Cylinder, after Étienne Bazeries, who later invented a similar device in 1891), used during late eighteenth-century conflicts and even later by the United States Army, for example, worked well but was not designed to be carried easily on one's body, to be portable and always accessible. Thicknesse describes a number of other inventions of the eighteenth century, too, that are useful, and arguably experimenting with screen technologies, but not bionic (in the sense that the Machina Cyclologica Cryptographica stylus could become part of the human body, enhancing its abilities). One device is a flat board fourteen inches long and twelve inches wide. Its middle is then carved out and lined with cloth, within which several sheets of foolscap paper (the size of today's legal-sized note pads – foolscap was less expensive and of lower quality than other papers) are positioned. A frame is then fastened around the edges of the paper, and a slide rule is attached to the lower part of the frame using springs. That slide rule is notched, and the reader must use their fingers to feel the notches and position the slide rule. Thicknesse's instructions are somewhat confusing, but he points out that such a device could also serve as a means of helping the blind learn to write. One of cryptography's more significant contributions to literacy, across the nineteenth and twentieth centuries, will be adaptive technologies for the disabled.

3.4 Sound Technologies

> A Bell no noise but *Rhetorick* affords;
> Our Musick Notes are Speeches, Sounds are Words.
> (West, 1641)

Richard West writes these lines in a poem that prefaces Wilkins's *Mercury*. His text brings historical attention to sound and its uses in secret communication, which he calls "cryptologia," or one of the most secret and swift forms of communication. In the opening chapter, Wilkins establishes that communication was first oral, with the ear the earliest "corporeal instrument" for "the *Receiving* and *Conveying* of Knowledge" and the tongue the "Instrument of *Teaching*" (Wilkins, 1641, 3). Near the end of his instructions, he positions musical ciphers as superior, providing examples. Thicknesse then tries to improve upon these. Thicknesse says that Wilkins's demonstrations lack harmony and rhythm and so are not really musical. If each letter does have its own sound, songs can be composed that can at once harmonize those sounds and communicate secrets. His example is of a music master who seduces a young woman; after teaching a young woman how to understand his musical alphabet, he can woo her in front of her parents. The *Treatise* is focused most intensely on musical ciphers as the superior approach, with long, detailed descriptions of possible methods and uses. He sees music to be the most secure for diplomatic correspondence, using the example of the Queen of Denmark, whose life is continuously in danger due to political factions. Her husband may be able to meet privately with various parties, but the Queen is sequestered and protected by so many layers of security that no correspondence could reach her – even to warn her of a threat. Yet, if the queen has been trained in a musical, harmonic alphabet, she can appear to play music "to divert her thoughts and employ her melancholy hours" but actually be communicating with allies, like her brother, outside (Thicknesse, 1772, 86–87).

The only shortcoming of secret communication through speech and music, Wilkins had acknowledged, is that the human voice cannot be heard across great distances without innovative technological mediation, and even if transported its messages would be too public for politics or business.[38] This limitation, he continues, in addition to the problem of permanence and perpetuation, is what prompted the invention of writing. This is precisely the problem that motivates Morland to invent devices like the *tuba stentoro-phonica* in 1670, a speaking trumpet made of glass or copper that was repeatedly tested and allowed the human voice to travel over a mile. Morland (1672) published on it in *Tuba Stentoro-Phonica, An Instrument of Excellent Use, As Well at Sea, As at Land*. Communication historian John Durham Peters has acknowledged that Wilkins proposed "a binary coding of the alphabet in visible or audible media," but he has mistakenly assumed that Wilkins's generation "had no idea of physical means such as the telegraph to send signals themselves" (Peters, 1999, 79).[39] Morland's communication device proves that we must be careful, as historians, to not assume technological ineptitude because of time period and underestimate the accomplishments of past thinkers. After first describing a series of successful experiments with trumpets of varying lengths, Morland includes a letter between Francis Digby and Lord Arlington, owners of two castles about a mile apart on the Kent coast that were built by Henry VIII as defensive forts. Digby and Arlington conversed with one another using the *tuba stentoro-phonica*:

> The first experiment I made, was between Waumer Castle and Deal Castle, with the disadvantage of a side Wind and some noise of the Sea, and yet we heard very distinctly from Castle to Castle, which are about a measured Mile asunder. Since that I have tryed the biggest of the three, which is turned

---

[38] Samuel Morland will prove Wilkins wrong on this point.

[39] Peters uses what he identifies as the third edition of *Mercury* dated 1707. I have not seen this edition.

Trumpet-wise, and when the Wind blows from the Shore, we hear plainly off at Sea as far as the Kings Ships usually ride, which is between two and three Miles. This we have done several times, but particularly some distance, we heard from the Castle, to Sir John Chichley's Ship, which lay in the best of the Road. So that without question, this will be of great use in all occasions where it's necessary to give Orders or Intelligence at a distance; but most of all at Sea, where we can give and take the advantages of the Wind, as is best for hearing. (Morland, 1672, 4)

Morland goes into detail about the physiological and mechanical engineering of the trumpets in his "A Short Discourse Touching the *Nature of Sounds*, and the manner how (as I conceive) they are magnified, or rather multiplied by the *Tuba Stentoro-Phonica*," the section following Digby's supportive letter. The discourse is rather overwhelming in its enthusiastic, even manic series of questions about the operations of sound waves and the ear:

But what manner of Images or Species such Percussions make; with such an infinity of distinctions and varieties? and how they fly about like Atoms in the Air? and are to be found in each point of the *Medium*? (and anon vanish into nothing?) and by what stupendious agility they are conveyed to the Soul? and how that does to receive so many millions of messages from without? and to dispatch and send out as many more from within? and in so short a space of time? the more we torment our thoughts about it, the less we understand it, and we are forced to confess our Ignorance. (Morland, 1672, 7)

Morland's interrogations are unique to his personal prose style and help readers map his thought process, which he always communicates clearly enough, and in such dialogue with the reader, that it is relatively easy to follow his logic. Narratively, he usually follows scientific questions like these with the apologetic conclusion that only God can know the answers. Then, however, he continues, as if calmed and refocused, to describe his own theory and the process through which he went to design, test, and perfect a machine or method. In answer to his own questions about sound waves, he discovers that a small tube of a very specific measurement, which widens based on a particular mathematical formula he explains, will successfully magnify as well as multiply the human voice. He then seems to step back to muse about what this new instrument might mean for the future of human communication, relating a narrative of 1615 by Bernard Varen, in *Geographia Generalis,* in which the author describes discharging a pistol a first time after having ascended one mile up Mount Carpathus in Hungary. This first shot does not produce much sound. Varen then walks down into the snowy woods and discharges a second time, and now the sound reverberates loudly and echoes through the dales a good half-hour. Despite his progress in understanding sound, this narrative puzzles

Morland. He believes his theory of percussion is the beginning of an answer, but he hopes that future scientists will take up the mystery more expertly. Closing his "Short Discourse," he does something uncharacteristic and humorously playful – he yells his final question in very large, bold, italicized, quoted font set off visibly from the rest of the page:

> *"What is that Right-lined, Curvy-lineal, or mixt*
> *"Figure? And what are its exact Dimensions?*
> *"And what the Sphere of its Activity? That*
> *"best and most magnifies Humane Voyce in*
> *"Syllables, Words, and Sentences?*
> (Morland, 1672, 12)

This moment of voice magnification via typographical manipulation not only expresses Morland's intellectual frustration – a frustration unlike him given his usual narrative ability to maintain empirical composure – but it also demonstrates the ability of *writing* to imitate sound to amplify human emotion.

Technologically, though, the potential of sound – the possibility of sending the human voice across miles and even farther, perhaps across the globe – is more exhilarating to him than the text-only cryptographic methods he shares in *New Method* and with his Machina Cyclologica Cryptographica. The examples he gives in the last section of his "Short Discourse" are emotionally moving. Not only can the trumpet be used to tell hostages that they will soon be saved, but it can also help coordinate citizens fighting a deadly fire in confusion, raise the morale of thousands of soldiers, organize hundreds of workmen, and send help when a family in the isolated countryside is being invaded by thieves. Even more exciting is the potential for such a device when it is used in combination with Morland's earlier cryptographic method, so that one could speak into it in an encrypted language. What emerges in these examples is Morland's philosophical and even humanist passion for the potential of a magnified human voice, for the achievements possible when communities are finally able to communicate and collaborate. As I note at the beginning of this Element, genres, practices, and even devices of secret communication are inspired by the desire for *connection* moreso than privacy or security.

3.5 Storage Devices

Cryptology prompts experimentation with writing and speaking instruments, surfaces, and mechanical devices, all needed for the encryption and decryption processes. Secret communication also requires technologies of storage as well. King Charles I's failed storage of ciphered personal letters in a chest that was seized at the Battle of Naseby revealed the dangers of not protecting secrets even after they had been delivered, read, and acted upon. The security of secret writing must be attended to long after its use. The recently studied locked letters in the Brienne Collection, a postmaster's chest of 2,600 undelivered letters sent from destinations around Europe to The Hague between 1689 and 1706, offers a contrast to Charles I's misfortune. Those letters have still not been opened, though that is more because of the circumstances of their delivery than the sophistication of their storage. Some were undelivered accidentally, others because the addressees were deceased or had moved. Those that are locked could have been opened if they were not being saved for preservation, though the purpose of some letterlocking was to reveal if a letter had been intercepted and broken into. This form of storage served more as an indication of eavesdropping than an impenetrable barrier.

As has been well documented by Barbara Benedict, Danielle Bobker, Maria Zytaruk, Paula Findlen, Lorraine Daston, Katharine Park, and others, the seventeenth and eighteenth centuries were periods fascinated by storage. Curiosity cabinets were means of collecting, organizing, classifying, and displaying – and I would add even hiding – one's most valuable belongings. They see the cabinets as new ways of categorizing knowledge and managing proliferating information, influencing a culture of epistemology. Closets are even more linked to secrecy. As Bobker finds, a closet is an "analogy for a hidden interior site" and often a place for "painful, shameful secrets" (Bobker, 2014, 73). Miruna Stanica studies pockets, trunks, bundles, bottles, cases, and boxes as they are represented in eighteenth-century literature, to posit that "these portable spaces of storage enable their human owners' mobility and action in the narrative, rather than sheltering them as domestic spaces do" (Bobker, 2014, 516). These highly functional spaces tend to be presented as lists of what they contain; these are inventoried spaces, not spaces for abstract contemplation or identity formation in the way that a home's interior space is presented. Stanica likens the inventory to a kind of diagram. The connections and meanings of those connections between objects in the pocket, for example, is not given but simply diagrammed; the listed objects serve as pieces of an identity, or situation, one must put together as observer. Like museums and curiosity cabinets, the list of a pocket's contents allows the objects to float in space as decontextualized, separate objects. The museum, cabinet, or pocket tells a story, but it is a story the observer must construct.

Inventories also become increasingly important in the storage devices used for bookkeeping. In the growing merchant class, businesses needed accounting books, ledgers, file cabinets, desks, and waste books to make their accounting transparent for creditors and debtors. Daniel Defoe (1726) describes several methods in *The Complete English Tradesman*, and John Mair (1741) provides a full instructional manual on bookkeeping storage strategies in *Book-keeping methodized*. Defoe describes an illiterate business owner who creates an elaborate, ciphered system (Defoe compares it to hieroglyphics) that only he can understand; he keeps separate drawers for each customer and detailed accounts of each day's business using notches on sticks, scores, symbols, and colors. The goal of some these genres of storage was not only to increase business efficiency but to convince others – like auditors – that one was *not* hiding anything, all while keeping data private. Yet, as industrial espionage became more common (a topic also discussed by Defoe), it did become helpful to hide some of one's business secrets, like recipes, designs, manufacturing plans, and craft practices. Defoe's tradesman must create a system that accommodates his illiteracy, but the secrecy of the system makes it a model for others. Growing businesses, and certainly the increased economic success of England as an empire, also necessitated the development of other kinds of innovations in storing secrets, namely safes (not made from fireproof metals until the nineteenth century), hidden spaces, and better padlocks. Some padlocks, like the word wheel, were clearly inspired by cryptography.

In a sense, cryptology is all about storage. Secrets must be concealed within ciphers, so that ciphers are themselves instruments of storage, and other methods are measured more or less against the security the encryption can provide. Thicknesse jeers at a ridiculous, failed experiment in storing secrets. "I cannot help mentioning a laughable experiment insisted upon by some, of bottling, as it were, up words in a tube, or trunk," Thicknesse writes, describing a desire commonly expressed in cryptology texts of the period that some storage instrument existed that could preserve or suspend the voice (Thicknesse, 1772, 106). After transportation, the bottle, tube, or trunk would be opened, and the speech would be released. Thicknesse also repeats the misconception that sound can in fact be frozen in cold climates. James Boswell repeats this same story in "On the New Freezing Discovery," republished in the *London Magazine* in August 1781 under the pseudonym "The Hypochondriack." Boswell, too, wished for a way to store the human voice.

Schott's (1665) *Schola steganographica* is an extraordinary visual work that emphasizes the importance of creative storage solutions for secret communication. Written in Latin, it provides interactive, unfolding illustrations and tables, such as a three-dimensional chest with compartments for characters of a cipher (see Figure 13). This might remind one of the first large computers that took up whole rooms, with cards that one moved to save and process data. The decipherer sorts the characters and deposits them into the chest, increasing efficiency with use.

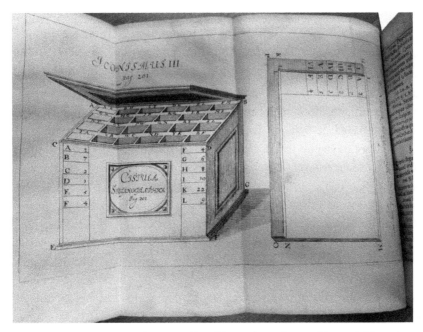

Figure 13 P. Gaspard Schott's (1680) illustration of a combinatorial box for secret writing in *Schola steganographica*. Courtesy of the National Cryptologic Museum

This chest, the Cistula Steganographica, is not just for saving or preserving messages; it is itself a reading device. It operates like a switchboard. Wooden sticks, upon which are written different sets of substitutions for letters, can be moved into slots for different letter groups according to the contract between sender and recipient. The operator can then move the sticks as needed, and as quickly as possible, to decipher different messages. It is much like the accounting method Defoe's tradesman will develop later.

Schott was a student of Athanasius Kircher (1663), who had been interested in cryptology in *Polygraphia nova et vniversalis ex combinatoria arte detecta*. Schott had certainly combined that inherited interest in secret communication with some of the creative mechanical ideas Kircher had imagined using storage boxes. *Polygraphia* had also featured a chest, which Schott replicates, called an *Arca seu cista steganographica*, or steganographic arc. In 1650, Kircher also diagrammed a series of boxes that functioned as musical machines. Users could insert small cartridges, which could play different kinds of sounds, in different compartments of the box. By simply rearranging the cartridges and putting them in different slots, one could create completely different songs. Storage becomes an act of multimodal communicative creation.

Technologies that interested cryptologists could increase efficiency, reduce error, and benefit the community in ways that go beyond secret writing. The field sparked interest in reading and writing instruction for the visually impaired, and also provided multimodal alternatives for the hard of hearing. Later systems of Braille develop out of this early work in communication, and the many experiments in visual and spatial ciphers and gesturing contributed to early sign-language systems. Devices like Morland's calculators and cipher wheels were usable for the physically disabled as well, simplifying otherwise physically arduous tasks – like writing out all of the numbers – to the act of reaching into one's pocket. Cryptologists also pointed out, repeatedly, that ciphering is a skill that does not require alphabetic literacy and thus opens a world of communication to those without the luxury of that education. Thicknesse describes a man who believed that putting on spectacles would allow him to read. When he still could not, his optician asked, "Whether he ever could read without spectacles?" (Thicknesse, 1772, 42). Indeed, he was illiterate, so this optical technology could not assist him. Learning cryptology, however, could.

4 Cryptotypographies

Cryptology publications reflected broadening notions of multimodal literacy during the long eighteenth century, contributing to advancements in access to literacy for the disabled and for those with less, or a different, education. They were also engaging self-consciously with the impact of print, even before the Restoration, and highlighting the ways in which writing did and did not change as the culture negotiated the relationship between script and print. As Elizabeth Eisenstein and others have argued, and as I discuss in *A Cultural History of Early Modern Cryptography Manuals* (Ellison, 2016), script and print worked in tandem throughout the early modern period; there was no clear demarcation between script and print culture. Even Trithemius's earlier *Steganographia* and *Polygraphiae libri sex*, published in 1518 after Trithemius's death in 1516, bridged oral transmission, scribal manuscript culture, and early printing. That hybridity and interdependence continued in cryptology instruction of the long eighteenth century. As I noted at the end of Section 1 on reading and writing processes, cryptography resisted the culture's growing dependence upon – and valorization of – alphabetic writing as sign of superior intellect. Though manuals of secret writing shared with other writing instruction this interest in cognitive materiality and visibility, cryptography resisted the assumption that the only written forms with power are alphabetic. The discipline also engaged reflectively with the standardization of visual form that print would motivate.

4.1 Cryptographic Space and Visual Habits

Cryptography instruction called out and challenged the visual habits that were becoming conventionalized with printing. In "The Art of Decyphering Discovered," the poet highlights how ciphered texts challenge readers' typographic expectations:

> Contiguous Words together blend,
> Without Beginning, without End. (Anonymous, 1727, 4)

Effective ciphers purposely play with the white spaces of the page, deleting and manipulating the distances that by that time were expected by readers. In one of John Falconer's examples, the first step in ciphering a message is to break down the conventions that make it efficiently read and understood by evenly spacing the letters and adding punctuation after each word instead of after each sentence. This is only one step in the process but, already, it significantly slows and complicates the reading process:

> I. s u p p o s e. t h a t. t h i n g s. a r e. s o. f o r w a r d. b y. y o u r. d i l i g e n c e.
> t h a t. w e. m a y. a d v e n t u r e. a t. a l l. o n c e. n e x t. w e e k. m e e t. m e. t
> o w a r d s. t e n. t o. m o r r o w s. n i g h t. a t. t h e. o l d. p l a c e. *b x y f q.*
> (Falconer, 1685, 52)

A next step, he observes, is often to then copy the message in a diagonal pattern, completely disrupting the typical linearity and direction of the reading and writing processes. Extraction following this process gives a writer a new message that might look something like this:

> I. g s y s. u t. o a p t. w u r p m a e. r. e. o t e l m d f s t o. e l. a l o. e h m t. o y. l f
> t e. o m n a i o h o r e. c d g r a l r t e. v e w t. d. o o n e n a t p w w e n c r h l s. a x t
> c. d. I a n r t. u t b n c I d w r h y. e. g s. e e. a *b* h t e a x t. e k. *y* a *n f*t. *q.*
> (Falconer, 1685, 53)

To solve a cipher of this nature, Falconer notes that one must think outside of the bounds of the standards of English writing and, as he demonstrates in the margin, outside the bounds of the typical printed page as well. One has to be able to imagine communication nonlinearly, in other kinds of patterns. In the far left-hand margin of this moment of instruction, outside of the block of maintext, he writes what may be marginal explication, though, without any explanation or connection back to the lesson (see Figure 14). While it is common for the instructional writers to include sources or notes in the margins, as other texts at the time did also, this is a rare moment that appears to be Falconer trying to clarify his own directions. However, if it follows the sequence that he outlines in the maintext immediately next to it, the placement of the letters is confusing.

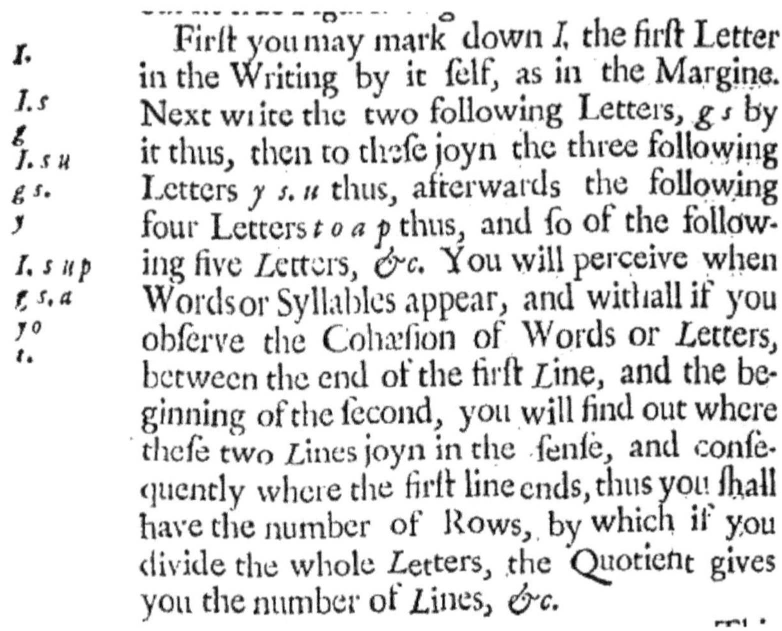

I.
I. s
f. s u
g s.
y
I. s u p
f s. a
y o
t.

Firſt you may mark down *I,* the firſt Letter in the Writing by it ſelf, as in the Margine. Next wiite the two following Letters, *g s* by it thus, then to theſe joyn the three following Letters *y s. u* thus, afterwards the following four Letters *t o a p* thus, and ſo of the follow‑ ing five Letters, *&c.* You will perceive when Words or Syllables appear, and withall if you obſerve the Cohæſion of Words or Letters, between the end of the firſt *Line,* and the be‑ ginning of the ſecond, you will find out where theſe two *Lines* joyn in the ſenſe, and conſe‑ quently where the firſt line ends, thus you ſhall have the number of Rows, by which if you divide the whole *Letters,* the Quotient gives you the number of *Lines, &c.*

Figure 14 Marginal explanation on page 54 of John Falconer's (1685) *Cryptomenysis Patefacta.* Courtesy of the National Cryptologic Museum

Rather than elucidate the complicated process he is describing, it further muddies it. Perhaps a serious student of cryptology would take this marginal annotation as a challenge.

In other examples, white space and the visual placement of characters are more intentional and better described. Cryptologists highlight how white space can be manipulated to protect messages, as Falconer shows, and also stress how when it is *not* manipulated, it can contribute to the insecurity of messages. This is because reader knowledge of syntax and grammar as represented by white space is more sophisticated than one may think – even if unconscious of how much one relies upon spatial cues to read, the mind still makes informed suppositions. In a number cipher that Falconer shares and that I reference earlier (see Table 4 with corresponding words and Table 6 for numbers alone), one can look at the word length and spacing to make educated guesses about the limited possibilities for several of the words. The first word is likely, though not definitely, "the," and other three-letter words can be discriminated as articles, conjunctions, or verbs based on the length of the words near them. Two-letter words also have a limited set of possibilities, like "at," "as," "to," "is," "it," "be," "go," and so on. Presenting this cipher without the formatted spaces, cryptologists note, would be wisest for its transportation.

Table 6 Cipher in John Falconer's (1685) *Cryptomenysis Patefacta* in which the numbers 436 are repeated but white spaces between words allow decipherers to test patterns

4	3	6	4	3	6	4	3	6	4	3	6	4	3	6	4	3	6	4	3	6	4	
3	6	4	3	6	4	3	6		6	4	3	6	4	3	6	4	3	6	4	3	6	4
4	3	6	4	3	6		3	6	4	3	6	4	3	6	4	3	6	4	3	6	4	
3	6	4	3	6	4	3	6	4		4	3	6	4									

Table 7 Cipher on page 36 of John Falconer's (1685) *Cryptomenysis Patefacta* that more effectively disorients typical reading practices

T	i	l	w	e	l	d	f	r	e
h	t	l	s	s	o	o	t	e	i
e	s	e	u	h	h	u	u	s	l
p	h	n	t	a	o	T	o	h	p
e	t	c	s	l	t	t	h	a	p
s	o	r	g	l	e	h	t	n	u
t	d	e	n	n	l	e	i	d	s
i	e	a	o	o	b	s	w	s	y
l	c	s	m	t	a	i	e	p	d
e	n	e	a	b	e	e	g	e	e

In other kinds of ciphers, the spacing can be manipulated into a kind of uniformity, and in a new order, that disorients the eye. Falconer demonstrates the visual adjustment needed to resist reading from left to right, descending (see Table 7).

To read this message in Falconer's instruction, one must read in the "ordinary way of writing amongst the Inhabitants of the Island *Taprobane, China,* and *Japan*," from the upper left corner and down the first column, then over one column to the right and up, then right and down, and so forth (Falconer, 1685, 36). Print allows Falconer to easily replicate and pass on this lesson at the same time that it challenges the reading pattern of the manual's own instructions.

4.2 Cryptology and the Hybridity of Script and Print

Cryptology instruction is also a clear example of the hybridity and interdependence of print and manuscript cultures. One of the simplest examples of print and script working together in secret communication is the popular example of the printed book upon which the edges are inscribed with a message if the pages are squeezed together in just the right manner. In other words, small marks that alone would not attract notice can be layered in such a way that they then line up to reveal meaning. This may require some rough handling of the book, even damage to its binding (Thicknesse, 1772, 100).

It is in the interaction between the genres of the instructional manual and the epistle that Wilkins, Falconer, Davys, and Thicknesse most demonstrate the interdependence of script and print in cryptology instruction and, in addition, the hybridity of ciphering. The most commonly repeated lesson from Wilkins's *Mercury* uses what he calls a "biform" cipher, based on Bacon's biliteral cipher,

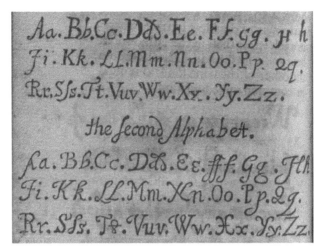

Figure 15 Two handwritten styles that can be used together in an epistolary cipher, called a biform cipher, in Wilkins's *Mercury* (Wilkins, 1641). This image is from the 1694 edition. Courtesy of the National Cryptologic Museum

which is two sets of alphabets in different handwritten styles. A decoy message is written in both alphabets, but only the letters in the style the correspondents have chosen should be copied down to reveal the solution.

In the key that Wilkins provides, the two styles seem straightforward enough: they are not so extravagantly different that a reader might figure them out instantly, but the first is less elaborate and has fewer flourishes than the second. Wilkins then provides a handwritten ciphered letter to demonstrate how the alphabets can be combined. Only the letters written in the more ornate, second alphabet should be copied to reveal the true message (see Figure 16).

The received epistle appears to affirm the recipient that the sender is doing well and does not need help. The reader, however, knows that only the letters with the flourishes should be read. It is difficult, though, to apply Wilkins's key to the example. Only with the provided solution (Figure 17) can one begin to make sense of which alphabet is the first or the second, and even with that help some of the letters are questionable.

Falconer repeats Wilkins's example in *Cryptomenysis*, with the identical epistle and solution, but he demonstrates how a biform cipher can work not only in handwriting but also (less effectively) in print, using different typographic styles. Perhaps Falconer recognized the flaws in Wilkins's handwritten example and wanted to make the differences clearer to readers. The result, though, is a cipher that is rather *too* obvious about how it hides its message (see Figure 18).

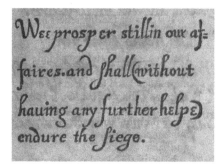

Figure 16 A message written in the two handwriting styles of the biform cipher in Wilkins's (1641) *Mercury*. This image is from the 1694 edition. Courtesy of the National Cryptologic Museum

Figure 17 The solution to the biform cipher in Wilkins's (1641) *Mercury*. This image is from the 1694 edition. Courtesy of the National Cryptologic Museum

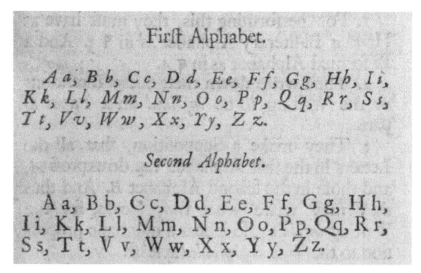

Figure 18 Two typographic styles in the biform cipher Falconer (1685) demonstrates in *Cryptomenysis Patefacta*. The plaintext is written in the first alphabet and the nulls are written in the second alphabet. Courtesy of the National Cryptologic Museum

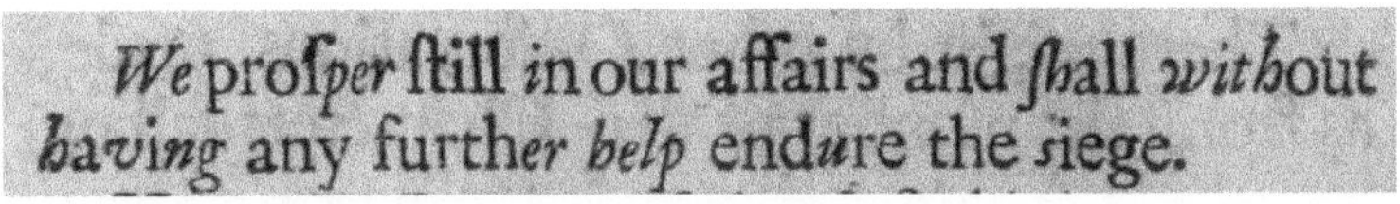

> *We* profper ftill *in* our affairs and fhall *without* having any further *help* endure the fiege.

Figure 19 Secret message written in two typographic styles in *Cryptomenysis Patefacta* (Falconer, 1685). Courtesy of the National Cryptologic Museum

In the example ciphered message, the reader can see that some letters are in the italic and some are not; the italicized letters should be copied down as part of the intended message to reach the same solution that Wilkins provides, "We perish with hunger help us." Falconer calls this method an "infolding" of one letter style within another, a term Bacon had used, in which one is exterior and the other is interior (Falconer, 1685, 84–85). Like Falconer, Thicknesse admires Wilkins's biform method but suggests that it is less effective than it would have been because "the publication of this art, in some measure defeated the use of it" (Thicknesse, 1772, 30). However, he acknowledges that it is still a strong method because it does not require that the recipient learn any special skills beyond recognizing when typographies or scripts are different.

Even more effective, Thicknesse believes, is one in which "proper" nouns – by which he means words written in all capital letters – indicate the tops of columns by which the words should be rearranged; in other words, it is a typographic scrambling technique one solves using a table. Like Falconer, Thicknesse shifts entirely to imitating through print rather than replicating handwriting. In the technical description in Figure 20, he experiments with visual layout.

Thicknesse uses what he claims is actual correspondence from the Earl of Argyle but, sadly, the cipher he provides is inaccurate. The simple method for deciphering it makes sense, but the sample texts do not work with his instructions. The reader who is following his steps would quickly see the error. I include it here as an example of a different kind of recategorization at the level of the word:

I gone so I and refuse object first you time much is way the our would have business very I possible of I send here against my 'till what little upon KNOW NOT which money assistance I service any what shall resolve THE at did least effectually thought requisite not sum truly this GROUNDS to say Mr. thing nor know they as hath grounds occasioned I do both do is red only let I distance in I half in an of thought my and go you in or resolved so I intend her or them OUR FRIENDS to neither to will much 'till any the know on in proposition could what other juncture I do mention this as as mean other I as neither give know offer HAVE. (Thicknesse, 1772, 28–29)

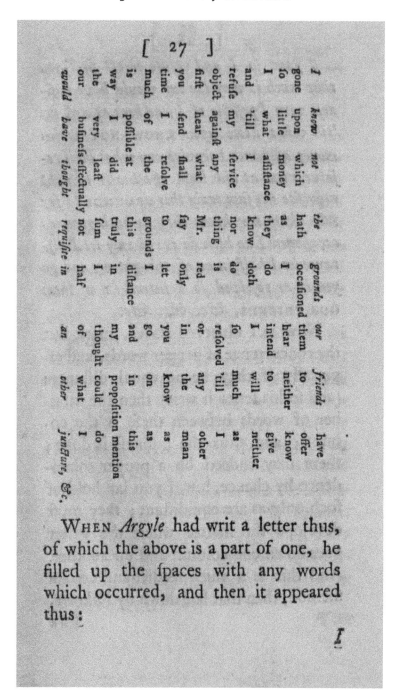

Figure 20 Visual layout experimentation in Philip Thicknesse's (1772)
*A Treatise on the Art of Decyphering and of Writing in Cypher. With an
Harmonic Alphabet*, page 27. Courtesy of the Library of Congress. Z103 .T42
Fabyan Coll

Decryption should, if it worked, reveal this message:

> I know not the grounds our friends have gone upon which hath occasioned them to offer so little money as I hear neither know I what assistance they do intend to give and 'till I know doth I will neither refuse my service nor do so much as object against any thing is resolved 'till I first hear what Mr. red or any other you send shall say only in the mean time I resolve to let you know as much of the grounds I go on as is possible at this distance and in this way I did truly in my proposition mention the very least sum I thought could do our business effectually not half of what I would have thought requisite in an other juncture, &c. (Thicknesse, 1772, 27)

Thicknesse is also interested in other kinds of reassemblage of text; for example, in rearranging the letters and words in printed literary works. He explains how correspondents might agree to use selections from Ellis Farneworth's (1762) printed translation of *The Works of Nicholas Machiavel* to provide a message written only in numbers that indicate where words are by which page, line, and word number, such as "page 7, line 2d, words three, four, and five; 2 vol. page 8, line 19, word 4, same page line 9; words 3, 4, and 5" which deciphered would say, "THE WESTERN EMPIRE IS DEGENERATED INTO LICENTIOUSNESS" (Thicknesse, 1772, 112). In this way, then, he relies in creative ways on the very material form of the printed text and its formatting, using the deictics of the book as object to locate the correspondent. Secrets are hidden in the conventions. For Thicknesse, this exploitation of the properties of print is a lesson in literacy. One should be confident that no matter how complex a writing may appear, if one approaches it with a method, and with awareness of the conventions of the media they look at every day, they can carefully work through it. The more difficult a cipher might appear, the easier it may actually be to solve.

More's (1716) *Of the First Invention of Writing* further illustrates the inter-secting interests of print and script in secret writing instruction. As noted in the introduction, More includes a short section on cryptography in his publication, but throughout this *printed* work he emphasizes the cognitive importance of writing by hand. His example alphabets are similar to Wilkins's but with more artistic skill, revealing that Wilkins was likely mimicking penmanship manuals of his own generation. As Goldberg finds in seventeenth-century writing instruction, More foregrounds the hand and its digits, where the hand functions not merely as a tool but as an extension of the mind. Writing must be a full-body experience, in More's view. Exercise of the hand is exercise of the mind, and both can become stronger and more skillful with practice. Even the smallest physical alterations or influences on the body, too, can dramatically impact one's ability to think and express themselves: "The Pen too hard, or too soft, or not fitted to the Hand, interrupts the Spirit and Power of the Action. The Ink too fluid or too thick. The Seat too high or too low. The false Light, or the Light too great, and a thousand other Impediments are so many Rubs in the Way of Dexterity" (More, 1716, 8).

An anonymous poem, "Mantissa," is appended to the end of More's *First Invention*:

> Tell me what Genius did the *Art* Invent,
> The lively *Image* of a *Voice* to *Paint*?
> Who first the Secret how to *Colour Sound*,
> And to give *Shape* to *Reason* wisely found,
> With *Bodies* how to cloath *Ideas* Taught,
> And how to draw the *Picture* of a *Thought*.
>   (More, 1716, 10)

The poet emphasizes the physical participation of the body in the expression of secrecy, and hands perform a range of types of mark-making, from painting to coloring, shaping, and drawing. And this sentiment is then captured in this print poem included within his instructional manual. An exercise in calligraphy that he provides, too, is a striking hybrid of script and print. This printed demonstration of calligraphy uses the medium of publishing to continue to advocate for developing aesthetically (and professionally) attractive penmanship in secret communication. Thicknesse's later lessons, which compile the highlights of manuals like Falconer's, highlight the peripheral skills necessary to notice small interventions of the hand in secrecy (see Video 4 for a demonstration) (Thicknesse, 1772, 103–106). In one of Thicknesse's example epistles, copied from Falconer's *Cryptomenysis* but with more thorough instructions, the message has been riddled with hand-placed dots that can only be revealed if the paper is dipped in water, sprayed with a particular chemical, or held up to fire. If the correspondents share the key in Table 8, they can use a range of methods to cipher their messages.

With the key, a sender writes the plaintext message that they want to cipher and align it with the numbers from the key, as shown in Table 9.

Table 8 Cipher key in Philip Thicknesse's (1772) *A Treatise on the Art of Decyphering and of Writing in Cypher*

a	b	c	d	e	f	g	h	i	k	l	m
4	22	10	9	1	11	13	18	3	19	12	8
n	o	p	q	r	s	t	u	w	x	y	Z
20	2	21	23	7	6	5	15	14	16	17	24

Table 9 Plaintext message in Philip Thicknesse's (1772) *A Treatise on the Art of Decyphering and of Writing in Cypher*

3	6	18	4	12	12	6	1	1	16	2	15	5	18	3	6
I	s	h	a	l	l	s	e	e	y	o	u	t	h	i	s
20	3	13	18	5	4	5	16	2	15	7	12	2	9	13	
n	i	g	h	t	a	t	y	o	u	r	l	o	d	g	
3	20	13	6												
i	n	g	s												

Video 4 Demonstration of the dot cipher in Philip Thicknesse's (1772) *A Treatise on the Art of Decyphering and of Writing in Cypher. With an Harmonic Alphabet.* Images used by permission of the Library of Congress. Z103 .T42 Fabyan Coll. Video available at www.cambridge.org/secretwriting

Now that each letter is represented by a number, the sender can draft a misleading message that appears to make sense and thus would escape suspicion. It does not matter what the message says as long as it is long enough. Figure 21 shows an example.

Hᴀᴠɪɴɢ underſtood that I could not be ſafe any longer where you are, I have choſen rather a voluntary baniſhment, to wander with my liberty abroad, than to lie under the daily hazard of loſing it at home. 'Tis in my opinion the leaſt of the two evils: 'tis true, I am innocent, but innocence is not always a buckler, ſo that I hope you will not condemn, even though you cannot approve, my choice ; at leaſt 'till you have the particu- lars of my caſe, which expect per next.

Figure 21 Cipher that would escape suspicion in Philip Thicknesse's (1772) *A Treatise on the Art of Decyphering and of Writing in Cypher*. Courtesy of the Library of Congress. Z103 .T42 Fabyan Coll

At first glance, there is nothing discernibly suspicious about the epistle. The writer claims their innocence and is banishing themselves voluntarily to save face. When the letter is held up in front of a flame or dipped in water, however, faint dots begin to emerge (see Figure 22).

The letters that these marks are placed beneath do not matter – what matters is the number of positions at which the marks appear. From the beginning of the message to the first mark, there are three letters. From that mark to the next (if we correct Thicknesse's mistake in leaving out the mark under the first "d" in "understood"), there are six letters. There are then eighteen letters to the next mark, and so on. The recipient must record each of these numbers to reach the numbered cipher (3 6 18 4 12, etc.).[40] When one then matches the numbers to the key in Table 8, the true message revealed is:

> I shall see you this night at your lodgings.

Earlier cryptology instruction, like Wilkins's *Mercury* and Gustavus Selenus's *Cryptomenytices et cryptographiae libri IX* (1624), inspired eighteenth-century

---

[40] Note that in addition to the missing mark in the first line, Thicknesse also neglects to finish out the full message needed to reach the end of the solution. He does not mention that he cuts the message short; perhaps, he assumes a reader will understand the method and then move on. A fully correct, operational cipher may not be necessary for the instruction.

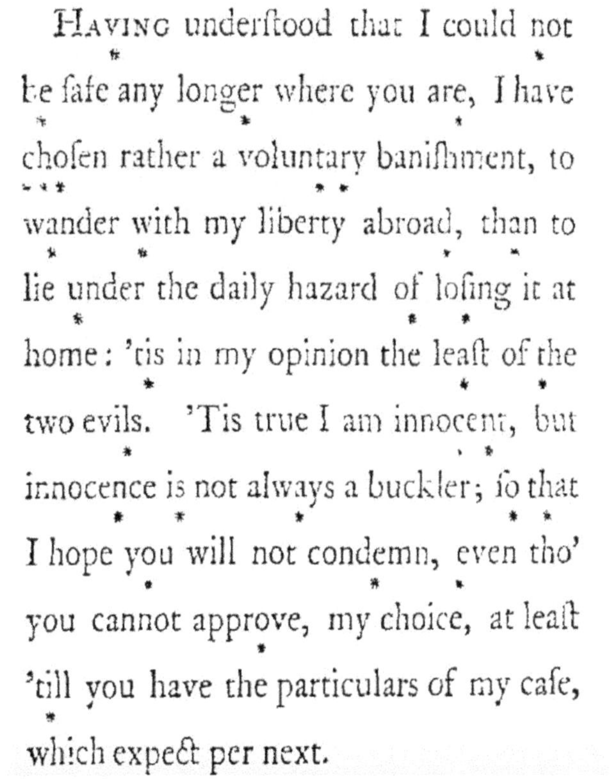

Having underſtood that I could not
be ſafe any longer where you are, I have
choſen rather a voluntary baniſhment, to
wander with my liberty abroad, than to
lie under the daily hazard of loſing it at
home: 'tis in my opinion the leaſt of the
two evils. 'Tis true I am innocent, but
innocence is not always a buckler; ſo that
I hope you will not condemn, even tho'
you cannot approve, my choice, at leaſt
'till you have the particulars of my caſe,
which expeſt per next.

Figure 22 Cipher with marks that are revealed with chemical or visual manipulation in Philip Thicknesse's (1772) *A Treatise on the Art of Decyphering and of Writing in Cypher*. Note that there is a mistake in this example: there should be a mark below the "d" in "understood" in the first line. Courtesy of the Library of Congress. Z103 .T42 Fabyan Coll

cryptologists to think multimodally in their print interactions with their readers. It was common for the instructional texts to feature not only experimentation with script and print but also multimodal demonstrations in the visual arts, architecture, and music. Selenus walks readers through how to use various kinds of shapes, images, gestures, and even textures in ciphers, highlighting the limitless possibilities for secret communication. He then includes a detailed pastoral image in which readers must notice the spots on apples, the eyes of birds in the sky and the laborers in the fields, and other marks to arrive at a solution. It is the final exercise in discernment – what is part of the cipher and what is not?

Selenus is here copying a dot cipher system he had seen in a hunting illustration in Johann Walch's *Decas fabularum humani generis* (1609). Even if they do not successfully complete the exercise, readers can clearly witness the

Figure 23 An illustration in Gustavus Selenus's *Cryptomenytices et cryptographiae libri IX* (1624) that acts as a kind of final exam in observation. Courtesy of the National Cryptologic Museum

bigger point here: that secret communication can be and is embedded in everything, that anything can be as expressive as alphabets, and that opening a world of secrets requires opening one's sensory field to recognize the expressive potential of all modalities. This is all captured in a printed book, which has a unique ability to bring them together.

Printing helped cryptologists legitimize the field as a reputable discipline worthwhile of study and use in politics, diplomacy, military situations, and even academics. They needed to circulate copies of instructional texts to promote their methods, even as the demonstration of those methods often had errors or ineffective typographic equivalents of nuanced handwritings. As evidenced by the intertextuality of the eighteenth-century texts, which reference a wide range of previous and contemporary publications on the subject, cryptologists also relied upon print to learn the field and build from the lessons of figures like Trithemius, Selenus, Wilkins, and Falconer.

4.3 The Pleasure of Printing Secrets

Just as the acts of ciphering and deciphering were described as gratifying, even erotic in their addictive challenges, so, too, were the printing and publication of instruction in secret writing a source of pleasure for cryptologists. Wilkins stresses that he publishes his methods not for the "publique good" but for the Stationer, for his profit, and for his own "delight" (Wilkins, 1641, "To the Reader"). It is not only enjoyable to share secrets but enjoyable to share *how* one shares them. Cryptology of the period is always highly self-reflexive. Carolyn Vellenga Berman makes an interesting point that shorthand writing, which would become popular alongside ciphering, promised to introduce new innovations in printing, pushing the industry to adapt because of its reliance on a wider range of linguistic symbols and grammars. Arguably, as these texts reveal, that was already happening. Yet, "rather than revolutionizing print language," Vellenga Berman continues, "modern shorthand generated a sensuous experience of all reading systems – and, indeed, all languages – as arbitrary and infused with political history" (Vellenga Berman, 2020, 74). In other words, shorthand – and I would argue secret writing instruction more broadly – reminded readers of the pleasure of the physical act of writing as it involves the body, and the senses, and as it can take advantage of a range of instruments and materialities. That experience is not specific only to alphabetic writing, or to the standards or traditions of a narrow definition of what writing and reading are or can be.

In their resistance to audience dependence upon print and the habits that writing for and reading in print created, cryptologists of the long eighteenth century challenged what texts *looked* like and how they could be used. Their advocacy for a graphically literate culture is demonstrated in many of the cipher exercises; readers are instructed on how to widen their peripheral vision, to see parts of texts that otherwise would be ignored, and to manipulate texts with their hands and bodies (even smelling and tasting them), through activities like folding, cutting, and burning. They explored the creative ways that ciphering encouraged writing and reading as material acts of construction, modification, and destruction.

5 Conclusion: Pulling Back the Curtain of Secrecy

Typically, popular histories of secret writing move from Elizabethan ciphering to the spies of the Revolutionary War, excluding over 150 years of significant theoretical and cultural influence that cryptology had on literacy, on processes of writing and reading, and on the technologies and materialities of writing and reading. In the nineteenth century, focus seems to have shifted to short-hand writing. Vellenga Berman argues that shorthand would connect citizens to the workings of government because it mediated the processes and languages of government proceedings (Vellenga Berman, 2020, 59). V. D. de Stains writes in *Phonography; or, the Writing of Sounds* that "the future progress of short-hand is essentially united with that of religious and political reform, in which cause it exerts an influence as powerful as that of the press itself, with which it is closely united" (De Stains, 1836, 108). Shorthand would thus become central in writing reform of the nineteenth century. A related art, brachygraphy, or "narrow writing," also became more popular as a kind of "fast writing for the steamship age" (Vellenga Berman, 2020, 67). The need for speed, then, seems to have surpassed the need for secrecy. In a sense, though shorthand and narrow writing can be as inaccessible as ciphers if one does not know the methods, the interest in shorthand was also motivated by a need to *know* secrets rather than to keep them. Shorthand became popularized, in part, out of contempt of the ruling class; it was a way to be let in to ruling class processes and conversations. Yet, learning it was tedious and gradual – it did not live up to its promise as fast and accessible for even the illiterate. This was the same for cryptography before it.

If Georg Simmel was right in his 1907 essay on secrecy, and the late seventeenth and early eighteenth centuries ushered in an era of political openness and transparency required for the emergence of a functioning democratic state, that disclosure created the very conditions upon which secret writing thrived. The more public government operations were demanded to be, the more creative those officials needed to become in order to communicate with one another and with citizen confidants. Private citizens demanded education about methods that state officials might use to deceive them; yet, they also wanted to protect their activities. Printing allowed readers to access instructional texts that catered to these demands and to the paranoia that Bernard Porter describes in his work on early espionage. Some of the authors of these secret writing manuals were already dabbling in cryptography and found a receptive audience for their knowledge, while other authors chose the topic in order to capitalize on the new market.

The sociological analysis of secrecy has been helpful in identifying its social importance as a construct and as an organizing community concept, yet it is also limited in its sensitivity to historical change and cultural uniqueness. Koen Vermeir and Dániel Margócsy note that while much work has been done on the content of the secrets – what exactly was being protected – less attention has been paid to the concept of secrecy as a "dynamic social relation" (Vermeir & Margócsy, 2012, 160).[41] For example, they challenge the "founding myths of science" as openly shared and for the public good – in contrast to technology, which is secretive – and theorize that during the early modern period, scientific secrecy became a tool of hierarchical social organization. Certainly, a glance at the ciphered correspondence of Robert Boyle and others would affirm this. Yet, the motives of that secrecy are not simple or binary; natural scientists were not simply hiding their work to protect it from theft or even theological condemnation but navigating a complex new communication system as yet without convention, in which the management of information, and the sharing of ideas, needed to become locally and globally strategic. Thinkers were operating in the midst of what Vellenga Berman calls "rapidly modernizing connective technologies," though she locates that development a century later during the Victorian period, when shorthand writing became more popular (Vellenga Berman, 2020, 81). Notably, a social skill necessary in the clearly increasingly global connectivity of the eighteenth century was the ability to be cautious of the trust of others. Disconnection, in this sense, is necessary for more meaningful connection. Secret writing allows authors to move through communication channels strategically, diverging (or, diverting, subverting) and converging with more control.

For Vermeir, cryptography is an example of the hybridity of secrecy and openness that challenges Pamela O. Long's positioning of them as opposites (Vermeir, 2012, 175). For Long, secrecy is intentional concealment; a lack of knowledge alone is not secrecy, though there can be secret things, which are unknown.[42] The distinction, for Long, when knowledge is unfamiliar, is that there is no active process keeping those things from being known. Privacy, as

---

[41] Koen Vermeir and Dániel Margócsy, "States of Secrecy: An Introduction" *The British Journal for the History of Science*, 45(2) (June 2012): 153–164, 160.

[42] This counters Samuel Johnson's understanding of "secret" in his *Dictionary*. There, he acknowledged three definitions: as the intentionally hidden, as a thing unknown or undiscovered, or as an invisible or undiscovered state.

protection from unwanted access by others, is counter to openness, as the relatively free access to information for particular audiences. Vermeir looks to seventeenth-century thinkers, however, to problematize this framework; for example, when Kircher used machinery behind the scenes in dramatic performances, he would reveal the apparatus only to elite audiences. This shows, for Vermeir, how early modern thinkers strategically controlled audience and access to create different degrees of secrecy and openness. Certainly, the cryptology texts do something similar. They, too, pull back the curtain to the special effects of codes and ciphers, exposing the step-by-step machinations of their workings. Similarly, Michael McKeon argues that public and private were not oppositional but separate social categories in *The Secret History of Domesticity*. His key example is from Wilkins's *Mercury*: he cites an opening dedicatory poem in praise of Wilkin's cryptography instruction to show how public and private could operate within the same discourse. In that poem, Richard West observes that "Secrecie's now Publish'd; you reveal/By demonstration how wee may Conceal" (Wilkins, 1641). McKeon notes that this reveals the "paradox of the publication of the private" and "an unusually reflexive exemplar of this truth" (West, 2006, xxii). This was not only the case in *Mercury* but across the genres of secret writing instruction.

Also helpful in Vermeir's cultural history of secrecy is further categorization of types, though secret writing instruction does operate across them. Esoteric methods of secrecy include traditions that create norms, such as warnings against exposure in order to prevent betrayal or arguing that revelation would damage the field or the craft. These kinds of flags become genre formulas, or even rhetorical conventions, that are not supposed to be questioned. In turn, they create elitism in which some readers will be included and some excluded based on their knowledge of the conventions. Theatrical methods of secrecy, exemplified by Kircher's performances, toyed with levels of openness (Vermeir, 2012, 181). In mathematics, theatricality was common. Results could be revealed with bravado, or in some cases, the writer would proceed only so far into their solutions and then leave a problem unsolved. For Vermeir, cryptography and secret writing fit within the third category of secrecy, the allegorical. "Cryptography, extensively studied in the seventeenth century, aimed at a rather straightforward coding and decoding of content," Vermeir writes, "although it was embedded in a complex culture of secrecy" (Vermeir, 2012, 185). Vermeir finds that cryptography poses secrecy as a "challenge" (Vermeir, 2012, 175).

This Element has tried to prove that cryptography of the long eighteenth century was not "rather straightforward" but was, certainly, playing a significant role in the culture of secrecy, specifically in its changing ideas about literacy and the processes through which readers interpret meaning. Even with algorithmic thinking, understanding of the expansive possibilities of categorizing and assembling language in creative new ways, and detailed attention to patterns and peripheries, readers still face a final challenge: they may reach the plaintext, but they still have to interpret the *meaning* of it. Cryptographers of the eighteenth century are careful not to conflate decryption and *interpretation*. The poet of "The Art of Deciphering Discovered: In a Copy of Verses to a Lady" emphasizes this at the end of their verse: the lady may follow the exact instructions in the poem to decipher the romantic epistle, but "fathoming the whole Intent" is the harder task (Anonymous, 1727, 8). Unless she can "apply't," she will not be able to interpret "*what* and *who* is meant" (Anonymous, 1727, 8). Reading in cryptographic contexts, then, requires being able to focus in, categorize, disassemble, find patterns in the secret, and recombine to form an intelligible message as well as focusing back out on the whole to consider the broader context.

Thicknesse uses the example of Egyptian hieroglyphics: the reason they have not yet been solved, he explains, is because his culture is unfamiliar with Egyptian religious practices. Cultural knowledge is necessary in order to fully decipher. He notes that even one's own language, from a century earlier, may seem like a hidden secret and thus requires research to understand. He provides an example of King William Rufus, who during a rebellion issued a proclamation that "those of his subjects who neglected to repair to his camp, should be reputed *Nidings*" (Anonymous, 1727, 78). Immediately, citizens from across his kingdom sped to his side, overwhelming the rebels. Why his announcement was so provocative was difficult for historians to fathom, Thicknesse notes. Yet, it was the word "Nidings" that had motivated them. Thicknesse says that his own culture does not understand what this word means (and Thicknesse does not define it for his reader). "Niding" means, generally, that one is obsolete, a despicable coward, or spiritually even that they have only a faint soul and so are nearly "nothing" (niding appears to come from the earlier word "nithing"). It is a term of emasculation and contempt, reserved only as an ultimate insult. Without this context, a reader cannot even understand their own history.

This brief volume attends not only to the rhetoric of secrecy and to strategies for hiding and revealing, as Vermeir and Margócsy as advocate, but to the ways in which that rhetoric, explicitly recorded in these intentionally crafted and printed cryptological publications, revealed a new way of thinking about literacy just as print was redefining reading and interpretation. While Benedek Láng doubts the influence of instructional cryptography texts, this Element, I hope, proves that these lively books are reflective of changes in how the culture thought about its composition processes, facilitating – and making *visible* – algorithmic thinking as a way of teaching writing. Some of these instructional texts, too, would influence practice well beyond their generation. The recent declassification and release of documents in the William F. Friedman collection and the John Matthews Manly Papers, in combination with resources in the George Fabyan collection at the U.S. Library of Congress, reveals that several of the texts discussed in this Element were "rediscovered" during World War I and used to train the first U.S. cryptanalysts – many of whom were literary scholars, who then took those reading practices back to their university departments to reform both writing and reading pedagogy. The instructional texts of this lost period of cryptography thus influenced writing and reading practices of the early twentieth century and a new era of surveillance and computing.

References

Akkerman, N., ed. (2011). *The Correspondence of Elizabeth Stuart, Queen of Bohemia*, 3 vols. Oxford: Oxford University Press.

Anonymous. (1727). The Art of Decyphering Discovered: In a Copy of Verses to a Lady, Upon Sending Her an Ænigma, Written in Cyphers. London: Printed for Step. Fletcher.

Anonymous. (1665). *Rarities: Or the Incomparable Curiosities in Secret Writing*. London.

Bender, J. & Marrinan, M. (2010). *The Culture of Diagram*. Stanford: Stanford University Press.

Bobker, D. (2014). The Literature and Culture of the Closet in the Eighteenth Century. *Digital Defoe: Studies in Defoe and His Contemporaries*, 6(1), 70–94.

Bok, S. (1984). *Secrets: Concealment and Revelation*. Oxford: Oxford University Press.

Braganza, V. M. (2022). "Many Ciphers, although but One for Meaning": Lady Mary Wroth's Many-Sided Monograph. *English Literary Renaissance*, 52(1), 124–152.

Bridges, N. (1659). *Stenographie and Cryptographie: Or, the Arts of Short and Secret Writing*. London: J. G. for the Author.

Britland, K. (2014). Reading between the Lines: Royalist Letters and Encryption in the English Civil Wars. *Critical Quarterly*, 55(4), 15–26.

Bullard, R. (2016). Secret History, Politics, and the Early Novel. In J. A. Downie, ed., *The Oxford Handbook of the Eighteenth-Century Novel*. Oxford: Oxford University Press, pp. 137–154.

Bullard, R. & Carnell, R., eds. (2017). *The Secret History in Literature, 1660–1820*. Cambridge: Cambridge University Press.

Buonafalce, A. (2004). Sir Samuel Morland's Machina Cyclologica Cryptographica. *Cryptologia*, 28(3), 253–264.

Burke, P. (2016). *Secret History and Historical Consciousness: From Renaissance to Romanticism*. Brighton: Edward Everett Root.

Campbell, M. B. (1999). *Wonder and Science: Imagining Worlds in Early Modern Europe*. Ithaca, NY: Cornell University Press.

Charles I. (1645). *The Kings Cabinet Opened: Or, Certain Packets of Secret Letters and Papers, Written with the Kings Own Hand, and Taken in His Cabinet at Nasby-Field, June 14, 1645*. London: Printed for Robert Bostock.

Collins, A. S. (1926). The Growth of the Reading Public During the Eighteenth Century. *The Review of English Studies*, 2(8), 428–438.

Cowan, B. (2018). The History of Secret Histories. *Huntington Library Quarterly*, 81(1), 121–151.

Cressy, D. (1980). *Literacy and the Social Order: Reading and Writing in Tudor and Stuart England*. Cambridge: Cambridge University Press.

Davys, J. (1737). *An Essay on the Art of Decyphering, in Which Is Inserted a Discourse of Dr. Wallis. Now First Publish'd from His Original Manuscript in the Publick Library at Oxford*. London: L. Gilliver and J. Clarke.

Deacon, R. (1969). *A History of the British Secret Service*. London: The Garden City Press Limited.

Defoe, D. (March 28, 1704). Mercure Scandale: Or, Advice from the Scandalous Club. *Review*.

      (1720). *Serious Reflections During the Life and Surprising Adventures of Robinson Crusoe: With His Vision of the Angelick World*. London.

      (1726). *The Complete English Tradesman, in Familiar Letters, Directing Him in All the Several Parts and Progressions of Trade*. London: Charles Rivington.

De Luca, E. & Haines, J. (2017). Medieval Musical Notes as Cryptography. In K. Ellison & S. Kim, eds., *A Material History of Medieval and Early Modern Ciphers: Cryptography and the History of Literacy*. New York, NY: Routledge.

De Stains, V. D. (1836). *Phonography: Or, the Writing of Sounds*. London: E. Wilson.

Douglas, A. (2017). *Work in Hand: Script, Print, and Writing, 1690–1840*. Oxford: Oxford University Press.

Dunton, A. (1705). *Dunton's Wit's Exercise*. London: Printed for the Author.

Eamon, W. (1994). *Science and the Secrets of Nature: Books of Secrets in Medieval and Early Modern Culture*. Princeton, NJ: Princeton University Press.

Eisenstein, E. (1982). *The Printing Press as an Agent of Change*. Cambridge: Cambridge University Press.

Ellison, K. (2016). *A Cultural History of Early Modern Cryptography Manuals*. New York, NY: Routledge.

Ellison, K. & Kim, S., eds. (2017). *A Material History of Medieval and Early Modern Ciphers: Cryptography and the History of Literacy*. New York, NY: Routledge.

Ezell, M. (2018). Multimodal Literacies, Late Seventeenth-Century Illustrated Broadsheets, and Graphic Narratives. *Eighteenth-Century Studies*, 51(3), 357–373.

Falconer, J. (1685). *Cryptomenysis Patefacta: Or the Art of Secret Information Disclosed without a Key*. London: Daniel Brown.

Goldberg, J. (1990). *Writing Matter: From the Hands of the English Renaissance*. Stanford, CA: Stanford University Press.

Goodey, C. F. (2011). *A History of Intelligence and "Intellectual Disability": The Shaping of Psychology in Early Modern Europe*. Surrey: Ashgate.

Jung, S. (2020). Reading, Visual Literacy and the Illustrated Literary Text in Eighteenth-Century Britain. In M. Hammond, ed., *Early Readers*. Edinburgh: Edinburgh University Press.

Kahn, D. (1996). *The Codebreakers: The Story of Secret Writing*. New York, NY: Scribner.

Kavey, A. (2007). *Books of Secrets: Natural Philosophy in England, 1550–1600*. Champaign, IL: University of Illinois Press.

Koscak, S. (2016). The Royal Sign and Visual Literacy in Eighteenth-Century London. *Journal of British Studies*, 55(1), 24–56.

La Fin, C. (1692). *Sermo Mirabilis: Or the Silent Language*. London: Printed for Thom. Salusbury.

Láng, B. (2018). *Real Life Cryptology: Ciphers and Secrets in Early Modern Hungary*. Amsterdam: Amsterdam University Press.

Long, P. O. (2004). *Openness, Secrecy, Authorship: Technical Arts and the Culture of Knowledge from Antiquity to the Renaissance*. Baltimore, MA: Johns Hopkins University Press.

Lupton, C. (2014). Gender and Materiality on the Eighteenth-Century Page. *Studies in English Literature, 1500–1900*, 54(3), 605–624.

Mair, J. (1741). *Book-Keeping Methodized*. Edinburgh.

McKeon, M. (2006). *The Secret History of Domesticity*. Baltimore, MA: Johns Hopkins University Press.

More, R. (1716). *Of the First Invention of Writing: An Essay*. London: Sold by the author, and by Major Hatley, and Mr Holland, in St Paul's Church-Yard.

Morland, S. (1666). *A New Method of Cryptography*. London.

(1672). *Tuba Stentoro-Phonica, An Instrument of Excellent Use, As Well at Sea, As at Land, Invented and Variously Experimented in the Year 1670, and Humbly Presented to the Kings Most Excellent Majesty Charles II, In the Year, 1671*. London.

Neocleous, M. (2002). Privacy, Secrecy, Idiocy. *Social Research*, 69(1), 85–110.

Neve, R. (1702). *Apopiroscopy: Or, a Compleat and Faithful History of Experiments and Observations*. London: D. Brown.

Oldfield, J. (1707). *An Essay Towards the Improvement of Reason; in the Pursuit of Learning, and Conduct of Life*. London.

Peters, J. D. (1999). *Speaking in the Air: The History of the Idea of Communication*. Chicago, IL: The University of Chicago Press.

Pepys, S. (2000). *The Diary of Samuel Pepys*, R. Latham & and W. Matthews, eds., vol. 8. Berkeley, CA: University of California Press.

Petty, W. (1674). *The Discourse Made Before the Royal Society . . . Concerning the Use of Duplicate Proportion*. London: Printed for John Martyn.

Porter, B. (1989). *Plots and Paranoia: A History of Political Espionage in Britain, 1790–1988*. New York, NY: Routledge.

Potter, L. (1989). *Secret Rites and Secret Writing: Royalist Literature 1641–1660*. Cambridge: Cambridge University Press.

Poynting, S. (2006). Deciphering the King: Charles I's Letters to Jane Whorwood. *The Seventeenth Century*, 21(1), 128–140.

Ratcliff, J. R. (2007). Samuel Morland and his calculating machines *c.* 1666: the early career of a courtier-inventor in Restoration London. *BJHS*, 40(2), 159–179.

Rider, R. E. (2020). Equations as Unruly Objects. *Nuncius*, 35, 471–505.

Schott, P. G. (1665). *Schola steganographica, in classes octo distribute*. Nuremberg.

Selenus, G. (1624). *Cryptomenytices et cryptographiae libri IX*. Lüneburg: Typis & impensis J. & H. der Sternen.

Sheffield, J. (The Duke of Buckingham). (1682). *An Essay upon Poetry*. London: Printed for Joseph Hindmarsh.

Simmel, G. (1950). *The Sociology of Georg Simmel*. Wolff, K. H., trans. Glencoe, IL: Free Press.

Stanica, M. (2014). Bundles, Trunks, Magazines: Storage, Aperpectival Description, and the Generation of Narrative. *Style: A Quarterly Journal of Aesthetics, Poetics, Stylistics, and Literary Criticism*, 48(4), 513–528.

Stewart, A. (1995). The Early Modern Closet Discovered. *Representations*, 50, 76–100.

Swaine, J. & Simms, J. (1761). *Cryptography: Or a New, Easy, and Compendious System of Short-Hand, Adapted to All the Various Arts, Sciences, and Professions*. London.

Taub, M. (2020). Sold: 53 Letters Deciphered by a Groundbreaking English Codebreaker. *Atlas Obscura*, www.atlasobscura.com/articles/john-wallis-cryptography.

Temple, W. (1701). *Select Letters to the Prince of Orange (Now King of England) King Charles the IId. and the Earl of Arlington, Upon Important Subjects*, vol. III. London.

Thicknesse, P. (1772). *A Treatise on the Art of Decyphering and of Writing in Cypher: With an Harmonic Alphabet*. London.

Usk, T. (1897). *Testament of Love*. W. Thynne, ed. Oxford: Clarendon Press.

Vellenga Berman, C. (2020). Tracing Characters: Political Shorthand and the History of Victorian Writing. *Victorian Studies*, 63(1), 57–84.

Vermeir, K. (2012). Openness versus Secrecy? Historical and Historiographical Remarks. *The British Journal for the History of Science*, 45(2), 165–188.

Vermeir, K. & Margócsy, D. (2012). States of Secrecy: An Introduction. *The British Journal for the History of Science*, 45(2), 153–164.

West, W. (1641). To His Honour'd Friend I. W. on His Learned Tract. In *Mercury; the Secret and Swift Messenger*. London.

West, S. M. (2018). Cryptographic Imaginaries and the Networked Public. *Internet Policy Review*, 7(2). https://policyreview.info/articles/analysis/cryptographic-imaginaries-and-networked-public.

White, J. (1704). *A Rich Cabinet of Modern Curiosities*. London.

Wiles, R. M. (1968). Middle-Class Literacy in Eighteenth-Century England: Fresh Evidence. In R. F. Brissenden, ed., *Studies in the Eighteenth Century*. Toronto: University of Toronto Press.

Wilkes, J. (1799?). *The Art of Making Pens Scientifically*. London: Printed by J. Vigevena.

Wilkins, J. (1641). *Mercury; or, the Secret and Swift Messenger*. London: I. Norton for John Maynard and Timothy Wilkins.

Cambridge Elements ⁼

Eighteenth-Century Connections

Series Editors

Eve Tavor Bannet
University of Oklahoma

Eve Tavor Bannet is George Lynn Cross Professor Emeritus, University of Oklahoma and editor of *Studies in Eighteenth-Century Culture*. Her monographs include *Empire of Letters: Letter Manuals and Transatlantic Correspondence 1688–1820* (Cambridge, 2005), *Transatlantic Stories and the History of Reading, 1720–1820* (Cambridge, 2011), and *Eighteenth-Century Manners of Reading: Print Culture and Popular Instruction in the Anglophone Atlantic World* (Cambridge, 2017). She is editor of *British and American Letter Manuals 1680–1810* (Pickering & Chatto, 2008), *Emma Corbett* (Broadview, 2011) and, with Susan Manning, *Transatlantic Literary Studies* (Cambridge, 2012).

Markman Ellis
Queen Mary University of London

Markman Ellis is Professor of Eighteenth-Century Studies at Queen Mary University of London. He is the author of *The Politics of Sensibility: Race, Gender and Commerce in the Sentimental Novel* (1996), *The History of Gothic Fiction* (2000), *The Coffee-House: a Cultural History* (2004), and *Empire of Tea* (co-authored, 2015). He edited *Eighteenth-Century Coffee-House Culture* (4 vols, 2006) and *Tea and the Tea-Table in Eighteenth-Century England* (4 vols 2010), and co-editor of *Discourses of Slavery and Abolition* (2004) and *Prostitution and Eighteenth-Century Culture: Sex, Commerce and Morality* (2012).

Advisory Board

Linda Bree, *Independent*
Claire Connolly, *University College Cork*
Gillian Dow, *University of Southampton*
James Harris, *University of St Andrews*
Thomas Keymer, *University of Toronto*
Jon Mee, *University of York*
Carla Mulford, *Penn State University*
Nicola Parsons, *University of Sydney*
Manushag Powell, *Purdue University*
Robbie Richardson, *University of Kent*
Shef Rogers, *University of Otago*
Eleanor Shevlin, *West Chester University*
David Taylor, *Oxford University*
Chloe Wigston Smith, *University of York*
Roxann Wheeler, *Ohio State University*
Eugenia Zuroski, *MacMaster University*

About the Series

Exploring connections between verbal and visual texts and the people, networks, cultures and places that engendered and enjoyed them during the long Eighteenth Century, this innovative series also examines the period's uses of oral, written and visual media, and experiments with the digital platform to facilitate communication of original scholarship with both colleagues and students.

Cambridge Elements$^{=}$

Eighteenth-Century Connections

www.ingramcontent.com/pod-product-compliance
Ingram Content Group UK Ltd.
Pitfield, Milton Keynes, MK11 3LW, UK
UKHW020454010325
455719UK00016B/585